Death and Resurrection:
Exploring the Mysteries of Suffering and Hope

By Elijah Lovejoy

Cover design: Sarah Ponzi, www.sarahponziarts.com

ISBN-13: 978-1537036748
ISBN-10: 1537036742

For Brandi

Who first learned to die
and rise with me

Table of Contents

Preface

Death and Resurrection: Exploring the Mysteries of Suffering and Hope describes events that happened between January 2008 and June 2010. After 5 years of reflection I began writing this book during the season of Easter 2015.   Much of my thinking for this work developed independently through study, reflection and conversation with friends. Three months before beginning the book, I read most of NT Wright's *Jesus and the Victory of God* and *The Resurrection of the Son of God*. These two works helped further develop my thinking about Jesus' death and resurrection as they relate to the new humanity Jesus is creating. *Death and Resurrection: Exploring the Mysteries of Suffering and Hope* is divided into three parts. Part 1 introduces the concept and implications of the death and resurrection cycle. Part 2 explores how Jesus uses death and resurrection to create a new humanity. Part 3 explores applications of the death and resurrection cycle for the world today.

I am grateful to my church, Church of the Redeemer, and my boss and friend, Rev. Alan Hawkins, for giving me time to write. I am also thankful to my family and church members who prayed for me, read the original manuscript and gave invaluable feedback that has shaped the book in your hands today. Last and most importantly, I am thankful to "God who raises the dead" (2 Corinthians 1:9). This book would not be possible without him.

Introduction: The Story of My Death

I grew up in a Christian home and always believed Jesus "rose from the dead on the third day," as the Apostle's Creed and New Testament teach. When I was 30 years old, I became the pastor of a new church start up in High Point, NC. Our chosen name, City of Grace Church, embodied a dream the church would be a beacon of God's grace to the entire city. We shared our homes, food and lives. We prayed for one another, worshipped together, served the community together and confessed our sins together. After 2 years, the church died.

People who visited the church remarked on its sweet atmosphere of love and warmth. At the same time fear and inadequacy were tightening like a boa constrictor around my heart. We needed to grow, but our marketing and personal invitations produced meager results. Our church was blessed with ethnic and socio-economic diversity, but I lacked the skills needed to bridge our differences. My prayers, sermons, outreach efforts and invitations to prospective members became increasingly desperate, as I watched the church plateau at 25-35 people over a two year period. Nothing bad happened. The church just died.

During a church leadership meeting, a team member could tell I was struggling and afraid. He asked a simple but disarming question. "Elijah, what's the worst that could happen?" Without pausing to filter my thoughts, I blurted out, "I could die. That's the worst that could happen!" Though my response was melodramatic, it captured the essence of what I feared. My dream of leading a church that would be a "city of grace" would die. What would I do vocationally, if this dream was dead? My professional reputation would die. Who was going to hire a pastor that killed a new church? My identity would die. Would I be known at gatherings of friends in ministry as "the guy who killed his church?" My financial security would die. How would my family survive after losing what was already a part-time income? My relationship with God would die. Did I not hear from God about pursuing this job? Was he playing a joke on me? Why did he not answer my prayers to save the church?

After a life of relative success including a state championship track title, graduating near the top of my class, winning a full scholarship to college and being praised as a stand out communicator and thinker, this was a stark and glaring failure. What would I do? How would I recover? Should I hide? Find another line of work? Lower the bar? Forget God? *Death and Resurrection: Exploring the Mysteries of Suffering and Hope* was birthed out of these questions and my desire to hear from God, especially through the Old and New Testament scriptures. The seventeen chapters and resurrection truths that follow are roughly chronological as I discovered them. They are also cumulative and build on one another. I offer this book to the church and the broader world for challenge, edification and encouragement. In particular I hope this book benefits people who feel death, loss, shame, suffering or failure have spoken the final word in their life. Let the journey of death and resurrection with Jesus begin.

Part 1: The Death and Resurrection Cycle

Chapter 1: Is Suffering Meaningless?

Resurrection Truth: Loss, suffering and death are not meaningless, but opportunities to die with Jesus.

"We always carry around in our body the death of Jesus."
2 Corinthians 4:10a

Many problems contemporary Christians face stem from viewing Jesus' death and resurrection as only one time events. Call this "the bookend theory" of death and resurrection. Death is the first bookend. Jesus died on the cross to forgive our sins and reconcile us to God. When we believe in him and confess our need for him, we are forgiven and our Christian life begins. His resurrection is the second bookend. When he rose from the dead, he showed his power and victory over death. When Jesus returns we will be raised from the dead and transformed to be like him. In between the bookends we seek to grow in faith, love and maturity.

It is true that Jesus' death and resurrection are onetime events. Romans 6:9 affirms, "For we know that since Christ was raised from the dead, he cannot die again; death no longer has mastery over him." It is not true that our death and resurrection are onetime events. 2 Corinthians 4:10 proclaims, "We always carry around in our body the death of Jesus, so that the life of Jesus may also be revealed in our body."

"Always." This haunting word burrowed deep into my soul. I was fighting valiantly to avoid City of Grace Church's death. But Paul was saying Jesus' death is not a one-time event in people who follow Jesus. It is something "we always carry." This led to a new thought. What if the death of this church was an opportunity for me to "carry around in [my] body the death of Jesus?"

Pouring over the context of 2 Corinthians 4:8-9, Paul is writing about emotional and physical life situations where he sees Jesus' death and resurrection at work in his ministry. Physically he is "hard pressed on every side but not crushed," "persecuted but not abandoned" and "struck down but not destroyed" (v.8-9). Emotionally he is "perplexed but not in despair" (v. 8). Paul then writes verse 10, not as a standalone abstract truth. It is the culminating lens through which he views and summarizes his life and ministry.

If this verse is true, it will change our life. All our suffering, loss, fears, failures and experiences with death are not badges of shame, reminders of our inadequacy and "the worst that could happen." They are opportunities to "carry around in our body the death of Jesus." A financial death of bankruptcy, relational death of betrayed friendship, emotional death of an unrealized dream, professional death of terminated employment, marital death of divorce and physical death of a lost child are not meaningless, unbridled suffering. Somehow all these experiences of loss are summed up in Jesus' death and provide an opportunity to carry his death in our body.

For the first time I started to believe God might have a mysterious purpose for the death of our new church. I wasn't joyful, but I was no longer hopeless. I didn't like the outcome, but I no longer believed God had completely abandoned me or I had completely abandoned him. I also began to read Scripture in a new way. If death and resurrection with Jesus was the culminating lens through which Paul viewed the Christian life, we should expect to find this pattern elsewhere in Scripture. I did.

The prodigal son rebelled against God and his father. When he returned home and repented, his Father welcomed him and described his life situation with these words. "This son of mine was dead and is alive again" (Luke 15:24). Jesus himself describes what it means to be his disciple in similar terms. "Whoever wants to be my disciple must deny themselves and take up their cross daily and follow me. For whoever wants to save their life will lose it, but whoever loses their life for me will save it" (Luke 9:23-24). Peter regards Jesus' death as something we participate in through our death to sin. "He himself bore our sins in his body on the cross, so that we might die to sins and live for righteousness" (2 Peter 2:24).

As exciting and hopeful as the truth of participating in Jesus' death is, it does raise a new question. Is dying with Jesus the end of our story?

Chapter 2: A New Rhythm of Life

Resurrection Truth: Jesus creates a cause and effect relationship between our death and resurrection.

"We always carry around in our body the death of Jesus, so that the life of Jesus may also be revealed in our body."   2 Corinthians 4:10

"So that." This was the second haunting phrase from 2 Corinthians 4:10. Not only is Paul's physical and emotional suffering an opportunity to "always" carry Jesus' death in his body. Paul also sees a causal ("so that") relationship between his experience of Jesus' death and Jesus' life in his body. Cause and effect logic shows up again in 2 Timothy 2:11 with the statement, "If we died with him, we will also live with him."

Perhaps the most detailed causal relationship between loss and gain, death and resurrection occurs in Philippians 3:7-11:

> [7]But whatever things were gain to me, those things I have counted as loss for the sake of Christ. [8] More than that, I count all things to be loss in view of the surpassing value of knowing Christ Jesus my Lord, for whom I have suffered the loss of all things, and count them but rubbish *so that* I may gain Christ, [9] and may be found in Him, not having a righteousness of my own derived from the Law, but that which is through faith in Christ, the righteousness which comes from God on the basis of faith, [10] *that* I may know Him and the power of His resurrection and the fellowship of His sufferings, being conformed to His death; [11] *in order that* I may attain to the resurrection from the dead (italics mine).

In verse 8b Paul regards himself to "have suffered the loss of all things, and count them but rubbish *so that* I may gain Christ." The causal relationship between loss and resurrection continues in v. 10 with "*that* I may know Him" and v. 11 with "*in order that* I may attain to the resurrection from the dead."

Some people are called to serve Jesus by leaving everything (Peter, James, John, the rich young ruler, St. Francis, and many leaders from church history!). Others are called to serve Jesus by staying home (Lazarus, Mary, Martha, Peter's mother-in-law and the Gerasene demoniac).[1] But all Christians are called to suffer loss for the sake of Christ, set aside their personal rights and take up their cross daily, in order that they may gain Christ and attain to his resurrection from the dead. Paul is not a virtuoso show-off, bragging about his suffering and loss to the church while others watch. He is a servant of Christ modeling death and resurrection, so the church can imitate him. The only difference between death and resurrection in Paul and us is one of degree. Jesus chose to apply death and resurrection through one set of circumstances to Paul. He will apply death and resurrection through a different set of circumstances to us.

On one hand the cause and effect relationship between death and resurrection should be obvious. We cannot be raised from the dead unless we first die. We cannot be healed unless we are sick. We cannot be found unless we are lost. We cannot repent unless we have erred. Jesus says, "Unless a grain of wheat falls into the earth and dies, it remains alone; but if it dies, it bears much fruit" (John 12:24).

On the other hand, the causal relationship between death and resurrection with Jesus is quite disturbing. What if the very

---

[1] NT Wright, *Jesus & the Victory of God*, p.298: NT Wright helpfully overviews varying levels of "summons" Jesus gives in his ministry.

thing I was fighting passionately to avoid (the death of a church and the suffering of my reputation) is the thing God wanted to use to raise me from the dead? What if my definition of "the worst that could happen" to my new church was God's instrument for my participation in Jesus' resurrection? What other areas of my life were motivated by fear, self-protection and avoiding death or suffering at all cost? How much of American culture (and by extension the church in America) is built on comfort, ease, convenience and the elimination of suffering and death? To what degree does our cultural avoidance of suffering and death keep us from experiencing (in this life and the life to come) the power of resurrection with Jesus?

In retrospect, all my frantic efforts to save City of Grace Church, though well-intentioned, were rooted in fear of death and hindered "the life of Jesus" from being revealed in my body. The truth of Jesus' causal relationship between death and resurrection started seeping into my soul. Life beats death. Resurrection beats crucifixion. Maybe the death of our church wasn't an eternal badge of shame, or even just an opportunity to carry Jesus' death in my body. Maybe this death was the prelude to resurrection with Jesus in some yet-to-be-revealed way. Maybe I wasn't called to sweep this unpleasant situation under the rug and never mention it again in polite company. Maybe I was called to embrace the cross with Jesus and look to the power of God to raise me from the dead.

Chapter 3: "Always"

Resurrection Truth: Jesus has made death and resurrection the pattern of the Christian life.

"I die daily." 1 Corinthians 15:31b

I knew our church was going to die. I knew in some mysterious way this was not meaningless suffering but an opportunity to carry Jesus' death in my body. I also believed this death was not the final word, but the prelude to resurrection with Jesus. The next question was obvious. Was this experience of death and resurrection a one-time event or the cyclical pattern of life Jesus always wanted for his disciples?

Jesus calls us to "take up [our] cross daily and follow him" (Luke 9:23). Paul says, "I die daily" (1 Corinthians 15:31) and "we always carry around in our body the death of Jesus" (2 Corinthians 4:10a). A person cannot die daily unless they are also raised from the dead daily. The cycle of death and resurrection with Jesus may be foreign to us. It was not foreign to Jesus or his apostles. In fact the static (or bookend) view of death and resurrection does a great disservice to Christians. We labor valiantly to live the Christian life between the bookends of Jesus' death and resurrection. Sadly, we often miss the power, comfort and hope of Jesus' death and resurrection rhythmically at work in the present.

Believing the cycle of death and resurrection with Jesus was "always" and "daily" at work in my life, I began looking for new ways this rhythm could bring power, purpose and hope to my life and the life of others. I especially looked for areas that seemed hopeless, shameful or beyond the power of God. What would resurrection look like in those areas?

First, the cycle of death and resurrection with Jesus shed light on seasons of life. At times we are in the rhythm of death. Later we find ourselves in the rhythm of resurrection. If resurrection is the culmination of the cycle for Jesus' followers, death will not have the final word. The lost job. The broken marriage. The deceased child. The dark night of the soul. These are all tragic and heart breaking experiences of death, but they are not hopeless. Because of Jesus they are the prelude to resurrection. This truth can't be spoken tritely. We can't place a time limit on our season of death. We can't guarantee how or when resurrection will happen or what it will look like. We should "weep with those who weep" (Romans 12:15) and not try to fix them. We should practice the Psalms of lament in our times of sorrow as Jesus did on the cross (Matthew 27:46; Psalm 22). But the Psalms, which contain a lament, "How long, O Lord? Will you forget me forever? How long will you look the other way?" (Psalm 13:1), also contain an expression of faith in God's goodness for the present and the future. "But I trust in your unfailing love; my heart rejoices in your salvation. I will sing to the Lord, for he has been good to me" (Psalm 13:5-6). Just as David recognized the Lord as sovereign over times of lament and confidence in Psalm 13, so we trust Jesus as Lord in seasons of death and resurrection. Death does not have the final word. Jesus has made death the vehicle of our resurrection.

Second, just as seasons of death ultimately lead to seasons of resurrection with Jesus, seasons of resurrection are followed by additional seasons of death. We can't freeze, control or manipulate the cycle. We trust and respond to the work of Christ in us, wherever he leads. Before discovering this cycle in the pages of Scripture, I viewed seasons or experiences of death with fatalistic pessimism. Here's another failure. I fell short again. I wonder how I'll recover this time. Now I started wondering the opposite. If I lost my job, my house, a child or was convicted of sin, as tragic and painful as these experiences would be, in the back of my mind I started to wonder what resurrection with Jesus would look like. I no longer feared the worst. I began to believe Jesus' resurrection in me would triumph, even if or when the worst happened.

Third, I began to search Scripture to see how resurrection with Jesus could be manifested practically in this life. Was resurrection from the dead only relevant after physical death, as the bookend theory holds? Should resurrection with Jesus cause us to expect anything for this life besides having faith and not being hopeless at funerals of brothers and sisters in Christ? After all, death is familiar to people inside and outside the church. Resurrection is the unknown and unexplored stranger. A lot could go wrong.

Again, the result was surprising. Paul regards Abraham and Sarah's conception of Isaac in the context of barrenness and old age as an experience of resurrection from the dead. "[Abraham] is our father in the sight of God, in whom he believed—the God who gives life to the dead and calls into being things that were not...Without weakening in his faith, he faced the fact that his body was as good as dead—since he was about a hundred years old—and that Sarah's womb was also dead" (Romans 4:17,19). The author of Hebrews considers Abraham's sacrifice of Isaac and receiving him back after God provided the lamb as a manifestation of death and resurrection in the present life. "By faith Abraham, when God tested him, offered Isaac as a sacrifice...Abraham reasoned that God could even raise the dead, and so in a manner of speaking he did receive Isaac back from death" (Hebrews 11:17,19).

Paul believes a severe test he faced in Asia is a fresh encounter with death and "God who raises the dead." "We were under great pressure, far beyond our ability to endure, so that we despaired of life itself. Indeed, in our hearts we felt the sentence of death. But this happened that we might not rely on ourselves but on God, who raises the dead" (2 Corinthians 1:8-9). Jesus describes the celebration, forgiveness and renewed life of a penitent sinner with his family as an experience of death and resurrection.[2] "We had to celebrate and be glad, because this brother of yours was dead and is alive again; he was lost and is found" (Luke 15:32). In the context of Luke 15, the rejoicing in heaven "over one sinner who repents" (v. 7, 10) is paralleled to the rejoicing over the younger son's resurrection from the dead. Heaven is not indifferent to the outworking of death and resurrection in our lives!

A natural question emerges from the passages above, and others like them. If Abraham, Sarah, Paul and the prodigal son could experience manifestations of death leading to resurrection in this life, why shouldn't all followers of Christ expect to find the same pattern at work in their life? In fact, I found this to be true and started anticipating a rhythm of death and resurrection in my life and the lives of people in my care. The death of my church led to a far healthier and more fruitful job at a nearby sister church. Around the same time, my wife's and my inability to have children for nine years gave way to a new baby girl. Hardships and character flaws which caused a dark season in our marriage were transformed by counseling and progressively developed into healthier ways of loving and relating. God was graciously blessing me with foretastes of resurrection in this life, which followed the rhythm of death and resurrection with Jesus. I knew I would face death and suffering again. In some areas of life I continue to face death. But now death operates in the service of resurrection--against the back drop of resurrection. I have nothing to fear.

I also began encouraging others to anticipate the pattern of death and resurrection in their life. I prayed for the death and

---

[2] NT Wright, *The Resurrection of the Son of God*, 437: I read NT Wright's similar analysis of the Prodigal Son's metaphorical resurrection in Luke 15 after writing this chapter.

resurrection of Christ to be at work in others who couldn't bear children (see Appendix 1 for a sample prayer I wrote). For people facing moral failure, I encouraged meditation on the rhythm of dying and rising with Jesus as he crucifies sin and raises righteousness from the dead. A down economy led to unexpected professional death for many friends who devoted their life to a company and were laid off. The cycle of death and resurrection with Jesus again affirmed that death does not have the final word in any area of life, including vocation. All encounters with death are excruciating. But Jesus' pattern of death and resurrection reframes our experience of death. I began seeing the pattern of death and resurrection everywhere in life and Scripture. I also began wondering why I was so afraid of my church dying.

Chapter 4: Why Are We Afraid?

Resurrection Truth: We fear death because we believe no better life exists than the one we've created for ourselves.

"I came that they may have life, and have it abundantly."
John 10:10

Fear is a good indicator of the extent to which we believe in resurrection. When City of Grace Church was dying I was full of fear. I feared disappointing people who supported me. I feared never getting a job in ministry again. I feared my reputation would die and never recover. I feared I was a fraud who couldn't hear from the Lord. Responding to this fear I frantically invited more people to join the church and invested in marketing strategies I hoped would stop the church from dying. Because I believed resurrection was only relevant for the life to come (see the "bookend theory" of resurrection from chapter 1), my only option was to protect the current life I had at all cost. Death was not an option. Death was bad, a sign of weakness and failure.

Through my fear, I could also empathize with other people's fear. The parent constantly worried about their child's health and safety. The company afraid of failure and risk. The religious skeptic deeply offended by the existence of suffering. These sentiments and the actions that follow from them made perfect sense in a world where resurrection has no contemporary relevance. If death and suffering are the worst that can happen, we must pursue control, security, elimination of risk and eradication of suffering at all cost. But if Jesus' words are true that "whoever wants to save their life will lose it, but whoever loses their life for me will find it" (Matthew 16:25), then death and suffering are not the worst that can happen. Seeking to save, protect and preserve our life, while missing resurrection with Jesus Christ, are the worst that could happen.

Like physical therapy releasing tension from a knotted muscle, Jesus' death and resurrection at work rhythmically in my life began to release months of fear, control and self-preservation bound up in my soul. If resurrection with Jesus is relevant for this life and the life to come, maybe fear, control and self-preservation weren't the only options. Maybe Jesus would somehow raise me and others from the dead, if we relinquish control of the life we created for ourselves and embrace dying and rising with him. Resurrection from the dead with Jesus opens new realms of possibility. If God can turn death, failure and suffering into new life and beauty, his options are literally endless.

Ironically, the church today often faces the opposite problem of the church at Corinth. Paul challenges the Corinthians, "If only for this life we have hope in Christ, we are of all people most to be pitied" (1 Corinthians 15:19). The Corinthians experienced amazing spiritual gifts, miracles, knowledge and growth in Christ during the present life, but saw little need to hope in Christ for the life to come. Rebuking the Corinthians, Paul affirms Jesus' resurrection from the dead is relevant for this life *and the life to come* when Jesus will raise our bodies from the dead. If Paul were to write the same challenge today, I suspect he would give the opposite rebuke. "If only for *the future life* we have hope in Christ, we are of all people most to be pitied." In other words, we need to rediscover that Jesus' death and resurrection are relevant to our future life, *but also to our present life.*

Jesus' death and resurrection worked out cyclically in the present also gives new insight into Jesus' ministry. NT Wright helpfully highlights the numerous challenges Jesus posed to his first century audience.[3] A partial list includes challenges to the following:

20

1. The temple ("Something greater than the temple is here." Matthew 12:6)

2. Family loyalty ("He who loves father or mother more than Me is not worthy of Me; and he who loves son or daughter more than Me is not worthy of Me." Matthew 10:37)

3. Care for the dead ("Follow Me, and allow the dead to bury their own dead." Matthew 8:22)

4. Money ("You cannot serve both God and money." Matthew 6:24)

5. The Sabbath ("The Son of Man is Lord of the Sabbath." Luke 6:5)

6. God's ethical commands ("You have heard that it was said, 'YOU SHALL NOT COMMIT ADULTERY'; but I say to you that everyone who looks at a woman with lust for her has already committed adultery with her in his heart." Matthew 5:27-28)

7. Israel's dietary laws ("Whatever goes into the man from outside cannot defile him, because it does not go into his heart, but into his stomach, and is eliminated? (Thus He declared all foods clean.)" Mark 7:18-19)

8. The right of self-defense (You have heard that it was said, 'AN EYE FOR AN EYE, AND A TOOTH FOR A TOOTH.' But I say to you, do not resist an evil person; but whoever slaps you on your right cheek, turn the other to him also." Matthew 5:38-39)

9. Worship ("Jesus said to her, "Woman, believe Me, an hour is coming when neither in this mountain nor in Jerusalem will you worship the Father." John 4:21)

---

[3] NT Wright, *Jesus and the Victory of God*, p.369-439: NT Wright's entire chapter, "Symbol and Controversy," helps explain the challenge Jesus' ministry posed to his audience in historical context.

10. Life itself ("He who does not take his cross and follow after Me is not worthy of Me." Matthew 10:38)

Each institution, command, symbol and person Jesus challenged above was central to the religious and societal life God had given Israel. To challenge and break all these life structures but offer nothing greater in their place would make Jesus a cruel anarchist. Consider this especially from Israel's perspective. After centuries of persecution, exile and oppression at the hands of foreign empires, the call and example of Jesus to die on Rome's instrument of torture (the cross), would have sounded bizarre, tone deaf and even sadistic. Surely Jesus offered something far greater along with his call to lose, diminish and die. Otherwise Jesus' original Jewish followers would have no reason to give up everything to follow him. Jesus and his apostles insist that for everyone who receives him, he is building:

1. A new temple ("Destroy this temple, and in three days I will raise it up." John 2:19)
2. A new family ("He said, "Who are My mother and My brothers?" Looking about at those who were sitting around Him, He said, "Behold My mother and My brothers!" Mark 3:33-34)
3. A new command ("A new commandment I give to you, that you love one another, even as I have loved you, that you also love one another." John 13:34)
4. A new covenant ("This cup which is poured out for you is the new covenant in My blood." Luke 22:20)
5. A new nation ("But you are a chosen people, a royal priesthood, a holy nation, God's special possession, that you may declare the praises of him who called you out of darkness into his wonderful light." 1 Peter 2:9)

6. New worship ("The true worshipers will worship the Father in the Spirit and in truth, for they are the kind of worshipers the Father seeks." John 4:23)

7. A new creation ("Therefore, if anyone is in Christ, the new creation has come: The old has gone, the new is here!" 2 Corinthians 5:17)

8. A new human ("Put on the new man, which in the likeness of God has been created in righteousness and holiness of the truth." Ephesians 4:24)

9. A new inheritance ("The Gentiles are fellow heirs and fellow members of the body, and fellow partakers of the promise in Christ Jesus through the gospel." Ephesians 3:6)

10. New wealth ("You know the grace of our Lord Jesus Christ, that though He was rich, yet for your sake He became poor, so that you through His poverty might become rich." 2 Corinthians 8:9)

11. A new city ("And I saw the holy city, new Jerusalem, coming down out of heaven from God, made ready as a bride adorned for her husband." Revelation 21:2)

12. New life ("I came that they may have life, and have it abundantly." John 10:10)

In fact reflecting on suffering and the future, Paul says, "I consider that the sufferings of this present time are not worthy to be compared with the glory that is to be revealed to us" (Romans 8:18). Similarly, reflecting on personal loss in the present, Peter says to Jesus, "Behold, we have left our own homes and followed You" (Luke 18:28). Jesus responds promising, "Truly I say to you, there is no one who has left house or wife or brothers or parents or children, for the sake of the kingdom of God, who will not receive many times as much at this time and in the age to come, eternal life" (Luke 18:29-30). Jesus sees our cycle of death and resurrection with him bearing fruit in this life and the life to come. A colleague helpfully observed that the promise of Luke 18:29-30 received initial fulfillment in the outpouring of the Holy Spirit at Pentecost, as new believers turned to Jesus and shared their possessions with one another, having all things in common (Acts 2:44-45).[4]

We fear death because we believe no better life can exist than the one we've created for ourselves. If death is the end, all threats to life should strike fear in our heart. If resurrection has the final word, why are we so afraid?

---

[4] Sarah Reid, a Church of the Redeemer colleague, shared this observation in conversation about the sharing of possessions at Pentecost being a fulfillment of Jesus' promise in Luke 18:29-30.

Chapter 5: Life Reconsidered

Resurrection Truth: If resurrection is inevitable, how would you live differently?

"Death no long has dominion over him." Romans 6:9

If Jesus is Lord over the death and resurrection cycle at work in our life, what can we learn from Jesus' original encounters with death and resurrection? Examining the gospel accounts of Jesus' last days, he predicts his death and resurrection three times on the way to Jerusalem (Mark 8:31; 9:31; 10:30-32). Jesus rarely predicted just death or just resurrection. He predicted them in combination. At times he seemed like a facilitator for his own death. This was going to happen. Judas, now is your cue to betray me (John 13:27). Peter, put your sword away (John 18:11). Pilate, I give you permission to murder me (John 19:11).

By his own words and actions, Jesus' death was inevitable. What about his resurrection? Jesus says, "I lay down My life so that I may take it up again" (John 10:17). "Destroy this temple, and in three days I will raise it up" (John 2:19). "You shall see the son of man sitting at the right hand of power, and coming with the clouds of heaven" (Matthew 14:62). If Jesus' death was inevitable, so was his resurrection. He lived what Hebrews 7:16 calls "an indestructible life." What could keep Jesus in the ground? Jesus' enemies had some ideas.

After Jesus was crucified and buried, the chief priests, Pharisees and Pilate did everything in their power to make sure Jesus stayed dead. Roman soldiers stood guard at the tomb. A stone covered the door. A seal fortified the stone. After Jesus rose from the dead, the chief priests paid a large bribe to the soldiers and concocted a lie that Jesus' body had been stolen (Matthew 28:12-13).

Money, lies, soldiers, a stone, the seal. None of it was enough to keep Jesus in the ground. As Keith Getty and Stuart Townend sing *In Christ Alone*, Jesus "burst forth in glorious day."[5] The chief priests and Pilate's efforts to keep Jesus in the tomb seemed silly compared to the power of God. An earth quake shook the ground. An angel rolled the stone away. The Roman guards became like dead men, paralyzed by fear (Matthew 28:2-4). Eye witness accounts of Jesus' resurrection exposed the chief priests' lie (1 Corinthians 15:3-8). Peter's sermon at Pentecost convicted and redeemed many who had cheered Jesus' crucifixion (Acts 2:37-41).

Jesus' disciples went from fearful men locked in a room after Jesus' death (John 20:19) to fearless heralds who celebrated being beaten for Jesus' name (Acts 5:41). The same religious leaders these disciples feared in John 20, they now boldly faced in Acts 5. What transformed their fear into boldness? The inevitability of Jesus' resurrection had changed everything.

Two new questions slowly emerged. Jesus' death and resurrection were inevitable. Nothing could keep him in the ground. I now carried Jesus' death and resurrection in my body by faith. If Jesus' resurrection was inevitable, is my resurrection also inevitable and what would this mean for my life?

2 Corinthians 1:8-11 provided helpful insight into the inevitability of resurrection. In the passage, Paul speaks of a near death experience he faced in Asia. Whatever the experience, it was "far beyond [Paul's] ability to endure" (v.8). Paul "despaired even of life" (v.8). He even "felt the sentence of death in [his] heart" (v.9). Paul is still alive writing this letter. We might expect him to conclude his story saying, "But everything turned out okay" or "It

---

[5] Keith Getty and Stuart Townend, *In Christ Alone*, 2001.

was a close call, but we made it out alive." Instead he says, "But this (the near death experience) happened that we might not rely on ourselves but on God who raises the dead" (v.9). Paul in essence says, "So what. Even if we had died, we serve the God who raises the dead."

My shift from seeing death as inevitable to viewing resurrection as inevitable was gradual but dramatic. Death has conditioned us a long time. It doesn't relinquish control easily. Adjusting to the inevitability of resurrection is a life-long battle and growth process. Several changes began to emerge.

First, all the emotional energy I spent protecting my ego, worrying about failure and warding off professional death, now seemed pointless. So what if I died? Jesus would raise me from the dead. A lot of what I feared needed to die anyway. Jesus didn't care about my ego, reputation or ability to climb a professional ladder. These were obstacles to his work in me, not assets. He wanted to kill what hindered God's work and raise me from the dead to a new life.

Second, as emotions like fear diminished, emotional peace and freedom grew. I could try new things and not fear failure. My ego didn't need constant protection. I wasn't responsible for creating and preserving my own life. Jesus was creating and preserving my life by his death and resurrection. Blunt honesty, criticism and conflict weren't the enemy. They were relational tools in service of resurrection with Jesus. The cycle of death and resurrection even emerged in Dr. Bruce Tuckman's team development stages commonly called, "forming, storming, norming and performing".[6] "Forming" paralleled creation. "Storming" paralleled death. "Norming" paralleled resurrection to a new

---

[6] Bruce Tuckman, (1965), "Developmental sequence in small groups," *Psychological Bulletin* 63 (6): 384–99.

reality. And "Performing" represented living out the new reality of resurrection with Jesus. Just as a team who refuses to "storm" hinders their own development, a Christian who rejects suffering and death opposes their own resurrection.

Third, I grew more content and excited about where I lived and worked. Prior to the death of our church, I had itchy feet. What was the next big thing I would accomplish, place I would move, person I would meet? Behind this restlessness was a desire to create my life, do something exciting, meet a need and move to greater heights. But the rhythm of death and resurrection with Jesus meant there was an endless amount of joy, work, depth and purpose God could accomplish in one place. I became content to serve and grow in my current location indefinitely. Jesus' call, not my itchy feet, became the deciding factor in where I would live and work.

Fourth, I began exploring the implications of death and resurrection for parenting. Children are naturally curious about death. They see something or someone die. They ask questions. Children also experience a death of the will when they're told "no" or experience discipline. The tears and wailing that follow demonstrate how real and difficult death is for them. A parent's tendency is to dismiss death, tell the child not to mention it and keep their child's will happy and content. But if Jesus has made death and resurrection the cycle of the Christian life, encounters with death provide an opportunity to teach kids at a young age about Jesus' work. Parents who avoid death just give their child more to unlearn later. Of course kids won't understand all the nuances of death and resurrection at age 5. But they should know death is not the end of the story. Jesus raises the dead both in this life and the next.

After five years of reflecting on the rhythm of Jesus' death and resurrection, I've only scratched the surface of its meaning for life. No doubt in some areas, I am blind to my own need for death and resurrection. As I grow and experience death in new ways, the backdrop will always be Jesus' inevitable resurrection at work in me. To Benjamin Franklin's famous words, "Nothing can be said to be certain, except death and taxes,"[7] Jesus adds a third certainty. "Nothing can be said to be certain, except death, taxes and resurrection."

---

[7] Benjamin Franklin, *in a letter to Jean-Baptiste Leroy,* 1789.

Chapter 6: Remembering True North

Resurrection Truth: God's ultimate goal is always life and resurrection, not suffering and death.

"Death has been swallowed up in victory." 1 Corinthians 15:54

If death inevitably leads to resurrection for Jesus' followers, why not seek death and suffering? Or in a variation on Paul's rhetorical question in Romans 6:1, "Shall we go on suffering so that resurrection may increase?" We have established that death and resurrection are the pattern of the Christian life. In this chapter we will examine the goodness of life and God's creation, which protect us from abusing the rhythm of dying and rising with Jesus.

I no longer believed the death of our church was meaningless. The Father had given me an opportunity to fellowship with Jesus in his sufferings and death, to carry his death in my body. Death was the necessary precursor to resurrection and could be used to serve the purposes of redemption. Jesus himself used death and suffering on the cross to redeem the world. He also warned in John 15:20, "A slave is not greater than his master. If they persecuted Me, they will persecute you also."

If death and suffering serve such redemptive purposes, should believers seek death out? Why care about life, family or the wellbeing of others? Shouldn't Jesus' followers seek to lose these things and welcome suffering, so Jesus can raise them to a new and better life? To put it bluntly, are suffering and death always good? To address this question, we must examine God's good creation, the entrance of sin into the world and Jesus' call to forsake our rights for the cause of his kingdom.

First regarding our sin, we should always seek its death. Scripture never speaks positively of sin or teaches us to let sin live.

Jesus says, "If your right hand causes you to sin, cut it off and throw it away" (Matthew 5:30). Colossians 3:5 exhorts, "Put to death, therefore, whatever belongs to your earthly nature: sexual immorality, impurity, lust, evil desires and greed, which is idolatry." Romans 8:13 affirms, "If by the Spirit you put to death the misdeeds of the body, you will live." Scripture never compromises with sin. Sin always must die, even though the battle will last a lifetime.

Second, Scripture generally doesn't command us to forsake our rights in the same way it commands us to kill sin. Rather forsaking our rights is a form of voluntary suffering modeled after Christ. For example Christ gave up his right to be served and instead washed his disciples' feet (John 13:14). Early followers of Christ gave up their right to a portion of their property and sold it for the common good (Acts 2:45). Paul encourages Christians at Corinth to give up their right to sue one another in court and instead suffer wrong (1 Corinthians 6:7). Paul has given up his rights to compensation for ministry, a believing wife and the freedom to eat whatever he desires (1 Corinthians 9:3-15). Jesus gave up a consistent place to sleep (Luke 9:58). Are all people required to give up these rights? Not necessarily, but Paul calls all Christians to have the same attitude of Christ who "emptied Himself, taking the form of a bond-servant" (Philippians 2:7). Dying to our rights for the sake of others is commended but not commanded.

Third, suffering and death within God's good creation require more discernment. Scripture teaches us to love life, care for our family, relieve suffering and seek healing when needed. Consider the ways Jesus and his followers seek to alleviate suffering in themselves and others. Jesus heals Peter's mother-in-law when she is sick with a fever (Matthew 8:14). Paul asks God three times to remove the thorn in his flesh (2 Corinthians 12:8). Jesus asked His Father to remove the cup of suffering from his lips (Matthew 26:39). Paul warned that anyone who neglects providing for their family "has denied the faith and is worse than an unbeliever" (1 Timothy 5:8). And when the invasion of Jerusalem begins, Jesus tells his disciples, "flee to the mountains" (Luke 21:21), not exactly a call to seek suffering.

As a result of these passages (and many others), we should not be passive or indifferent in the face of death and suffering. The bias of Scripture is always toward life and resurrection. Even before Jesus died and rose, God made creation good (Genesis 1:10). Women wanted to have children (1 Samuel 1:11). Sick people wanted to be healed (Luke 5:12). Jesus wept when his friend died (John 11:35). After Jesus' death and resurrection, life remains preeminent. Resurrection dominates the cycle. It has the final word. Resurrection is our destiny.

If life is created good and the saints of Scripture regularly avoid or alleviate suffering, why (besides dying to sin or voluntarily giving up our rights to serve others) does Jesus tell us to daily take up our cross (Luke 9:23) and to expect persecution (John 15:20)? Why does Paul say he is always carrying Jesus' death in his body (2 Corinthians 4:10)? Why does Peter call us to rejoice as we participate in the sufferings of Christ (1 Peter 4:13)? Why does James proclaim, "Consider it pure joy, my brothers and sisters, whenever you face trials of many kinds" (James 1:2)?

Jesus' death provides helpful insight for our understanding of death and suffering. On the one hand, Jesus didn't seek death out. He escaped situations where people wanted to kill him (Luke 4:30). He prayed to avoid death, if it was His Father's will (Matthew 26:39). He protected his disciples from death at the time of his arrest (John 18:8-9). And he cried out in anguish when he finally encountered death (Matthew 27:46). On the other hand, when Jesus knew that "the hour" (John 17:1) had come for his death, he embraced the cross and prayed for God to be glorified. He rebuked Peter, who used force to oppose Jesus' death (John 18:11). And he faced death with confidence he would be raised from the dead and ascend to His Father (Luke 9:51). Jesus' death was simultaneously ugly and beautiful, brutal and peaceful, wicked and just, shameful and glorious, weak and powerful, perverse and pure, hateful and loving, foolish and wise, deceitful and true.[8] We shouldn't be surprised to find the same multi-layered complexity at work in our own experiences of suffering and death with Jesus.

Like Jesus, our approach to suffering and death requires discernment and prayer. In the case of City of Grace Church, I wanted to see it live, grow and thrive, partly from pure and partly from impure motives. When growth didn't happen and death looked increasingly likely, I became frantic. Only through prayer, seeking the Lord and reading Scripture did I discern God was calling me to embrace death, something I never considered or wanted. Two good questions to discern when we should and shouldn't embrace death are these. Is the death or suffering I'm facing outside my control or reasonable ability to escape? Is the death and suffering I'm facing the result of irresponsibility, negligence, selfishness or self-martyrdom? God generally calls us to embrace death in the first scenario and rebukes our pursuit of suffering and death in the second scenario.

If my life is in danger, I will do everything in my power (except sin) to protect it. If my best efforts fail, and death becomes imminent, I will rejoice in the privilege to die and rise with Jesus. In other words, when followers of Christ face unavoidable physical or metaphorical death, they face a win-win scenario. The Apostle Paul beautifully summarizes this win-win reality in his letter to the Philippians. He is in prison preparing to face a Roman tribunal with

---

[8] Nathan Hedman, a Church of the Redeemer member, in conversation observed the cross' unique status as an instrument of great beauty and horror.

life or death consequences in the balance. From prison Paul writes Philippians 1:20-25 and reflects:

> [20] I eagerly expect and hope that I will in no way be ashamed, but will have sufficient courage so that now as always Christ will be exalted in my body, whether by life or by death. [21] For to me, to live is Christ and to die is gain. [22] If I am to go on living in the body, this will mean fruitful labor for me. Yet what shall I choose? I do not know! [23] I am torn between the two: I desire to depart and be with Christ, which is better by far; [24] but it is more necessary for you that I remain in the body. [25] Convinced of this, I know that I will remain, and I will continue with all of you for your progress and joy in the faith.

Paul is in chains awaiting trial. The decision of life or death is out of his hands. He is at peace with either outcome. Because of Jesus, life and death represent a win-win scenario for Paul. If given the choice, as he ponders how God will move, Paul prefers life. If given the same choice, we should prefer life as well.

Chapter 7: I Will Raise Him Up

Resurrection Truth: Death and resurrection serve God's purposes and cannot be manipulated.

"Lord, if You had been here, my brother would not have died."
John 11:21

As I grew more confident in the rhythm of Jesus' death and resurrection, I saw great personal potential. My 25-35 member church was about to die. Perhaps God would raise me from the dead with a 1000 member church. Or if I wrecked my 1999 Toyota Corolla, would God raise me from the dead with a new Z4 BMW? While Jesus' death and resurrection offer great power and encouragement, God will not allow us to use them for manipulative or selfish purposes. This would be contrary to the very nature of Jesus' death and resurrection. Selfishness needs to die, not be given new life.

If we cannot manipulate the power of resurrection for our purposes, what are God's purposes in our death and resurrection? Initially, I wanted God's purpose for the death and resurrection of our church to be my personal enrichment, vindication and fame (of course God would receive glory as well). God declined but had other ideas in mind. Scripture reveals at least 4 ways God is accomplishing his purposes in our suffering, death and resurrection.

First, God calls us to trust him in the timing of our death and resurrection. After their brother, Lazarus, died Martha and Mary said to Jesus, "Lord, if You had been here, my brother would not have died" (John 11:21,32). We can relate to Martha and Mary with an infinite number of similar "What if?" and "Where were you?" questions. In response to Martha Jesus makes a simple promise in v. 23, "Your brother will rise again." Martha replies, as we often do, by spiritualizing Jesus' words and making them true for the future, but not the present. "I know he will rise again in the resurrection at the last day" (v.24). Not until Jesus commands concrete action ("Take away the stone." v. 39) does Martha realize Jesus intends for resurrection to come crashing out of the future into the present. Jesus' words are fulfilled when "The dead man came out, his hands and feet wrapped with strips of linen, and a cloth around his face" (v.44). Resurrection came sooner than either Mary or Martha expected.

Other times resurrection delays, as in the case of the martyred souls in Revelation 6:10 who cry out, "How long, O Lord, holy and true, will You refrain from judging and avenging our blood on those who dwell on the earth?" God responds to their question in Revelation 6:11 that "They should rest for a little while longer, until the number of their fellow servants and their brethren who were to be killed even as they had been, would be completed also." Whether resurrection comes unexpectedly after we've made peace with death or delays longer than hoped, God calls us to trust his resurrection timing.

Second, God wants us not to fear suffering and death, but to flee from evil. Jesus' apostles taught early Christians to expect suffering and death. For example, 1 Peter 4:12-14 admonishes, "Beloved, do not be surprised at the fiery ordeal among you, which comes upon you for your testing, as though some strange thing were happening to you; but to the degree that you share the sufferings of Christ, keep on rejoicing, so that also at the revelation of His glory you may rejoice with exultation." In approximately 155 CE Justin Martyr, executed by beheading in 165 CE, famously wrote to Emperor Antoninus Pius, "You can kill us, but you cannot hurt us."[9] Of far greater concern to Justin Martyr than losing his life was

---

[9] Justin Martyr, *First Apology*, Christian Classics Ethereal Library, www.ccel.org.

being found guilty as an evil doer. He was also very concerned the Emperor would violate his own soul and be judged by God as an evil doer for killing innocent Christians. Justin Martyr was simply following the words of Jesus who said, "Do not fear those who kill the body but are unable to kill the soul; but rather fear Him who is able to destroy both soul and body in hell" (Matthew 10:28). Elsewhere when declaring all food clean, Jesus says:

> That which proceeds out of the man, that is what defiles the man. For from within, out of the heart of men, proceed the evil thoughts, fornications, thefts, murders, adulteries, deeds of coveting and wickedness, as well as deceit, sensuality, envy, slander, pride and   foolishness. All these evil things proceed from within and defile the man (Mark 7:20-23).

Jesus and early Christians cared far more about evil thoughts or deeds coming out of their heart than bodily suffering or death happening to their body. Today Christians often see suffering and death as unfair (How could a good and loving God allow suffering?), while viewing unclean thoughts and deeds that flow from the human heart with less concern.

Looking to the future, top scientific research on life extension and reverse aging treatment provides a helpful clarifying question. What will happen if scientists one day discover a cure for biological death without a solution for the evil deeds Jesus mentions flowing from the human heart in Mark 7:20-23? We would live in a world where our bodies could potentially live forever, but our heart remained as dark as before. Eternal life without a purified heart is no paradise at all. Death and resurrection teach us to care less about what happens to our decaying bodies, which Jesus will raise from the dead as new incorruptible bodies. Instead, we should flee the evil thoughts and deeds that corrupt both our body and soul.

God's third purpose for death and resurrection is to mature his people through suffering. Paul writes, "We also glory in our sufferings because we know that suffering produces perseverance; perseverance, character; and character, hope. And hope does not put us to shame, because God's love has been poured out into our hearts through the Holy Spirit, who has been given to us" (Romans 5:3-5). Elsewhere Paul experiences such severe suffering that he prays three times asking God to remove Paul's "thorn in the flesh." God responds, "My grace is sufficient for you, for power is perfected in weakness" (2 Corinthians 12:9). Once again Paul sees death and resurrection at work in his sufferings, "Most gladly, therefore, I will rather boast about my weaknesses, so that the power of Christ may dwell in me. Therefore I am well content with weaknesses, with insults, with distresses, with persecutions, with difficulties, for Christ's sake; for when I am weak, then I am strong" (2 Corinthians 12:9-10). We often want a quick and painless fix to our suffering and death. God is far more interested in perfecting his power in our weakness and purifying our heart from pride, selfishness and other evil deeds that make us unclean.

Fourth, God wants to cultivate contentment in us regardless of where we find ourselves in the death and resurrection cycle. Paul teaches the Lord's all pervasive purpose and presence in life and death. "For not one of us lives for himself, and not one dies for himself; for if we live, we live for the Lord, or if we die, we die for the Lord; therefore whether we live or die, we are the Lord's" (Romans 14:7-8). Jesus reminds Martha and Mary of a similar constancy in John 11:25-26, "Jesus said to her, 'I am the resurrection and the life; he who believes in Me will live even if he dies, and everyone who lives and believes in Me will never die. Do you believe this?'"

People who hear my story of death and resurrection sometimes ask, "What if you hadn't experienced resurrection? What if you weren't offered a new job, didn't have four children after nine years of infertility or hadn't experienced greater restoration in your marriage relationship?" Beyond these questions we could easily ask others. What about the cancer patient who suffers in pain for years? What about the child who grows up with a physically abusive alcoholic parent? Where is Jesus' resurrection in these situations? If I hadn't encountered resurrection, I hope I would still live with faith in the power of Jesus' resurrection at work in me, whether through strength or weakness, life or death. I came to believe in the rhythm of dying and rising with Jesus before experiencing any foretaste of resurrection. If I were currently unemployed, childless and divorced, I believe Jesus would still manifest his resurrection in the present and future in different ways. In each scenario above, whether in Scripture or our own life, God calls us to trust him. He is Lord of the death and resurrection cycle, not us.

Part 2: Death, Resurrection & Human Destiny

Chapter 8: A New Kind of Human

Resurrection Truth: The purpose of dying and rising with Jesus is to become a new human.

"If anyone is in Christ, that person is a new creation."
2 Corinthians 5:17

For five years I taught, reflected and marveled about Jesus' death and resurrection rhythmically at work in the life of believers. I watched hearts melt and faces streak with tears as people realized Jesus' death and resurrection was present in areas of life they had buried in shame, hopelessness or confusion. In my own life, I grew in depth, joy and peace, even facing trials that would otherwise have derailed me. But there was more.

Should we expect more from participating in Jesus' death and resurrection than bringing meaning and comfort to the life of individual believers? The death and resurrection cycle made sense of Jesus' ministry in the New Testament. It gave meaning to the failures, hardships and death believers experience but feel they must hide. It also created strong confidence in the ultimate victory of Jesus' resurrection in this life and the next. Most of these truths speak to the life experience of individual believers. They do not address God's global purposes for humanity and the universe. NT Wright's *Resurrection of the Son of God* revealed the more that God desires.

Wright views Jesus' permanent bodily resurrection from the dead as the beginning of a new humanity that God is recreating. According to Wright as he reflects on 1 Corinthians 12, "What the creator god has accomplished in and through Jesus is the renewal of the human race, that for which humankind was made in the first place. What better image, then, to use for its corporate life than that of a human body, with limbs and organs working as they were meant to do?"[10] About the Easter event more broadly Wright explains:

> For Paul, the point of the resurrection is not simply that the creator god has done something remarkable for one solitary individual (as people today sometimes imagine is the supposed thrust of the Easter proclamation), but that, in and through the resurrection, 'the present evil age' has been invaded by the 'age to come', the time of restoration, return, covenant renewal, and forgiveness. An event has occurred as a result of which the world is a different place, and human beings have the new possibility to become a different kind of people.[11]

Jesus' death and resurrection does not just give us a pattern for life. He has also given us the means of becoming a new kind of human race, progressively in this life, then definitively and completely in the resurrected life to come. As Romans 8:29 states, Jesus is the first perfected image of God, unlike the corrupted, sin-marred image in Adam, Eve and their descendants. He is the first new human, who will be followed by many other new humans conformed to his true image. "For those whom He foreknew, He also predestined to become conformed to the image of His Son, so that He would be the firstborn among many brethren" (Romans 8:29).

---

[10] Wright, *The Resurrection of the Son of God*, 295.
[11] Ibid., 332.

We often miss the truth of our new humanity in Jesus for two reasons. First we have spiritualized and made intangible many of the New Testament references to our new humanity in Christ. Second we don't understand God's original purpose for creating Adam, Eve and the entire human race "in the image of God." We will examine these misconceptions in order.

First, consider the New Testament's use of image and new human language from Genesis 1 and 2. Paul describes Jesus as "the image of the invisible God" (Colossians 1:15). According to Ephesians 2:15 Jesus is creating "one new man" that unifies Jews and Gentiles. In Ephesians 4:22-24 Paul admonishes believers to "lay aside the old man...and put on the new man." Colossians 3:10 speaks of "being renewed...in the image of the Creator." Elsewhere Scripture describes "a new creation," "a new birth," "[bearing] the image of the heavenly" and being "Christ's body and individually members of it" (2 Corinthians 5:17, 1 Peter 1:3, 1 Corinthians 15:49, 1 Corinthians 12:27).

Like the childhood body anatomy game Operator, new humanity language could be all abstract imagery and metaphors intended to teach and inspire us. One glaring fact makes the abstraction and spiritualization of new humanity language problematic. As the "firstborn from the dead" (Colossians 1:18), Jesus Christ has charted the path for his followers own resurrection, and the path is quite physical indeed. Jesus now reigns from heaven in his resurrected body, the first time in history a human-- our own flesh and blood--has ruled the universe. Why would Jesus' humanity, including his resurrected new body, be highly physical and our renewed humanity be only intangible, abstract and metaphorical?

The tangible nature of language describing "a new human race" in Christ challenges the complacency with which we often interpret biblical phrases such as "new creation, new man and renewed image." If Jesus' death and resurrection is rhythmically at work in us now, we should expect progressive growth in the goals of his death and resurrection. One such goal is to create a physical new human race, conformed to Jesus' new human image and united to him as one body. God's work of death and resurrection in us is intensely physical and intensely human.

Second, to understand God's purpose for creating a new humanity through Jesus, we must examine why God created the first humans "in the image of God" (Genesis 1:27). According to Bruce Waltke, bearing "the image of God" in the Ancient Near East (ANE) was the prerogative of kings, who ruled on behalf of the gods.[12] Being created in God's image conveyed moral authority to rule, royal representation of the deity and divinely entrusted responsibility over that deity's realm. In contrast to the king, according to numerous ANE creation stories, everyday humans were created by the gods to do hard manual labor, which the gods found distasteful and grew tired of performing.

When God created Adam and Eve "in the image of God" (Genesis 1:27) and commanded them to "be fruitful and multiply" as well as "fill," "subdue" and "rule" the earth (Genesis 1:28), he was calling them to join him as kings and queens in the work of shaping, cultivating and ruling the creation he had made. In essence, Adam, Eve and all their offspring are privileged by God to be sub-rulers, sub-creators and sub-caretakers of God's good creation, under his ultimate sovereignty. Unlike other ANE creation stories, which view everyday humans as slave laborers created to replace lazy grumbling gods, the Genesis creation story views all humans as kings and queens of God's creation. God walked with (Genesis 3:8-9), instructed (Genesis 2:17) and rested with (Genesis 2:2) his royal image bearers in the Garden of Eden.

---

[12] Waltke, *An Old Testament Theology*, 218.

When sin entered the world in Genesis 3, everything changed. The image bearers heart was darkened, knowing good and evil. They fled from God, their Creator. They felt shame and opened the gates of death. God exiled his image from the life-giving garden. Because we are created in God's image as his kings and queens of creation, to sin is not just to make a mistake or be a bad person. To sin is to misrule. It is to renounce the source of our life, purpose and authority. To sin is to cut ourselves off from the presence of God, who desires to walk and rest with us.

Bruce Waltke's explanation of "the image of God" within the ANE context and the perversion of that image by sin sheds new light on our need for a new human image bearer to renew us. God has not abandoned his purpose for humanity. Through Jesus' death and resurrection he is remaking new image bearers--new kings and queens--who will rule, care and create as God intended. This is why we must become a new human, a new creation, renewed in the image of God and conformed to the image of his Son. Image and creation language is not incidental to the work of Jesus in the New Testament. It is essential to Jesus' work as he eternally renews the image of God in humanity through death and resurrection.

A renewed teacher now serves, blesses and rules his class room as a Christ-conformed king. A Christ-bearing artist now creates her work with renewed awareness of Jesus' death, life and eternal glory permeating the universe. A newly created parent now shepherds his or her children relying on Jesus' death and resurrection to shape a new generation of kings and queens. Through our participation in his death and resurrection, Jesus the perfect image bearer, is now making us new human images of God to rule and care for a newly created universe.

Chapter 9: Why Gifts Will Cease

Resurrection Truth: Jesus' death and resurrection unleash spiritual gifts to build the new humanity.

"Christ gave the apostles, the prophets, the evangelists, the pastors and teachers, to equip his people for works of service, so that the body of Christ may be built up." Ephesians 4:11-12

Watching City of Grace Church die, I was alone. As a solo-church planter, I was the preacher, counselor, administrator, pastor, accountant, event planner and youth minister. I wasn't good at many of these roles, but it didn't matter. I was alone. What was missing? In retrospect I was missing the mutually-complimentary spiritual gifts found in a team environment.

In contrast to my church planting isolation, every time Paul mentions spiritual gifts in the New Testament, he always combines gifts with "body of Christ" imagery (Romans 12:4-5, 1 Corinthians 12:27, Ephesians 4:12). For Paul's audience, "body of Christ" language was not an abstract image disconnected from the person of Christ. "Body of Christ" had a very concrete reference point in the death and resurrection of Jesus. Why did Paul consistently frame spiritual gifts in the context of Jesus' resurrected body? And what role do the gifts play in the new human Jesus is creating?

Ephesians 4:7-16 powerfully answers these questions. The passage opens in v. 8 with a quotation from Psalm 68:18 and imagery of a king's triumphant return from battle. Upon victory, a king who conquered his enemies "ascended on high" and was enthroned to rule the defeated. Kings often displayed their glory and humiliated their captives (sometimes stripped naked) by marching them as slaves behind the king's triumphant procession back to his capital (2 Chronicles 36:20; Isaiah 20:1-6). After returning to his kingdom, a king imprisoned his captives or pressed them into hard labor. For his own people the victorious king shared his plunder, especially with loyal subjects who backed his reign. We continue this practice today in the words of early 19th century New York Senator William Marcy after the presidential victory of Andrew Jackson, "To the victor goes the spoils."

How does this battle imagery relate to Jesus' work, spiritual gifts and the building up of a new human race? Jesus' ascension, following death and resurrection, to the right hand of the Father demonstrates Jesus' glory, authority and victory in battle (Acts 2:33-35). Unlike militaristic warfare, Jesus waged war through his death on the cross against spiritual enemies far more powerful than any earthly king. Jesus' captives are death and Hades along with spiritually dark powers and principalities, which Jesus enslaved after his victorious resurrection and ascension (Revelation 1:17-18; Colossians 2:15; 1 Peter 3:21-22). The plunder Jesus took from these captives is their ability to kill, degrade and destroy God's good human creation. In the words of Colossians 2:15, Jesus "disarmed the powers and authorities, he made a public spectacle of them, triumphing over them by the cross." Jesus then gave spiritual gifts as the spoils of war, won through his triumphant death and resurrection. The purpose of these gifts is to labor with Jesus to build the new human race, the body of Christ. Jesus is the firstborn living, conquering, ruling embodiment of the resurrected human race. His enemies still seek to "steal, kill and destroy" (John 10:10), but through his death and resurrection Jesus has disarmed these enemies for all who trust in him.

After outlining what is commonly called the five-fold equipping gifts in Ephesians 4:11, Paul explicitly connects the purposes of the gifts to the building of a new humanity, a new body of Christ. God intends the gifts "to equip his people for works of service, so that the body of Christ may be built up until we all reach unity in the faith and in the knowledge of the Son of God and become mature, attaining to the whole measure of the fullness of Christ" (Ephesians 4:12-13). Continuing the new humanity language, Paul says in Ephesians 4:14-16:

> [14]Then we will no longer be infants, tossed back and forth by the waves, and blown here and there by every wind of teaching and by the cunning and craftiness of people in their deceitful scheming. [15] Instead, speaking the truth in love, we will grow to become in every respect the mature body of him who is the head, that is, Christ. [16] From him the whole body, joined and held together by every supporting ligament, grows and builds itself up in love, as each part does its work.

Jesus gives spiritual gifts so we can labor with him to fulfill our eternal destiny, being transformed into the fullness and perfection of Christ. At Christ's return, our purpose will be fulfilled and gifts will no longer be necessary. As NT Wright observes, this is why Paul can point in 1 Corinthians 13 to a time when gifts will cease while love remains.[13]

Jesus intends his followers to mature as new humans through mutual edification and relationship. He created the body of Christ, the church, as the context for believer's growth into the fullness of Christ. Each gift of teaching, mercy, encouragement, faith or leadership is essential to the work of new humanity. [14] Division, isolation and selfishness threaten the new humanity because they cut believers off from Jesus' body and gifts. Division and isolation degrade. Unity and interdependence nurture.[15]

---

[13] Wright, *The Resurrection of the Son of God*, 295-296.
[14] For a full list of spiritual gifts see: Ephesians 4:11, Romans 12:6-8, 1 Corinthians 12:27-28 and 1 Peter 4:10-11

Like an endless spring of water, Jesus' death and resurrection are the source of our new humanity and of the spiritual gifts we receive to build up that new humanity. What an honor. Jesus establishes the new humanity. Then he calls and empowers believers to co-laborer with him, advancing the work of redemption he has begun. Before our eyes Jesus is building tangible and eternal new humans through his church.

---

[15] Jesus and Paul's ardent prayers and exhortations toward unity take on new meaning in light of the building of the new humanity (1 Corinthians 3:1-9, 12:18-20; Romans 12:3-5; John 17:11).

Chapter 10: Death, Resurrection and Holiness

Resurrection Truth: God uses the cycle of death and resurrection to sanctify our new humanity.

"Count yourselves dead to sin but alive to God in Christ Jesus."
Romans 6:11

During the process of our church dying, my marriage was also dying. My wife and I were married seven years. We had much in common and got along reasonably well. About the seventh year we hit a wall. The smallest detail set off an argument. We believed the worst about each other's motives--they did that to hurt me, they don't care about me, their behavior is never going to change. We regularly had what one friend called "round the mountain conversations," the same conversation over and over with no noticeable progress. Our positions were entrenched. We had our list of self-justifications and attacks for why the other person's accusations were untrue or unfair and ours were correct. One person said we sounded like two lawyers facing each other in court. My wife sometimes asked if I was okay. I wasn't, but was emotionally lazy, so I said "yes." I preferred to lie and say everything was okay, than be honest, say I wasn't okay and engage in hours of emotional conversation, which I viewed as a painful waste of time. My wife wanted to go to counseling. I resisted.

When we finally started counseling, it was one of the hardest things I have done. Simultaneously facing death in our marriage and our church compounded my sense of dread and misery. Our counselor shared helpful truths that sustained our hope. First, God uses people and situations to "stir the pot" in our heart and bring attitudes, beliefs or behaviors to the surface he wants to address and heal. Second, emotions are often leading indicators of something happening at a deeper level in our life. In our brokenness, we looked for how God was stirring, and we paid attention to our emotions.

Each counseling session led to a week of painful self examination, honesty, listening and repentance between my wife and me. Emotionally, I felt like one body part after another was being chopped off. I wondered if I could continue living with so few body parts remaining. What was happening to my life? Jesus' death and resurrection were at work sanctifying my new humanity in at least three ways.

First, I had numerous unhealthy, self-righteous, self-protecting, sinful attitudes and behaviors that needed to die, so I could become a new human. God calls this process of being made a new human sanctification. His primary method for sanctifying believers is the cycle of death and resurrection which crucifies sin and resurrects us with new Christ-formed attitudes, habits and behaviors.

In retrospect, every period of sanctification in my life has involved a process of dying and rising with Jesus. In middle school, I died to my desire for popularity and rose to a hunger for pleasing God. In high school, I died to my self-righteousness and rose to a constant dependency on Jesus as my Savior. In marriage, I died to my emotional laziness and self-protection and rose to Christ-centered forgiveness and truth. In the death of my church, I died to my ego and rose to follow Jesus who "did not come to be served, but to serve" (Matthew 20:28). Romans 6:6-7 says, "For we know that our old self was crucified with [Jesus] so that the body of sin might be done away with, that we should no longer be slaves to sin--because anyone who has died has been freed from sin." No doubt, I will die and rise with Jesus many more times as he continues my sanctification. The cycle of death and resurrection can be painful. It should not be surprising.

Second, God was leading me through a similar process Jesus faced in his temptation. Jesus was stripped down and weakened by fasting. Then he was tempted by Satan in three specific ways. Finally, he emerged victorious from his testing. Many Christians who follow the Church Calendar will be familiar with this pattern of fasting from the Season of Lent.[16] Even for Christians who don't follow the Church Calendar, the story of Jesus' temptation (Matthew 4:1-11) contains important truths for Christian sanctification.

Anyone who has fasted for a period of time, especially from something they love, can attest to the strain fasting causes. Fasting from coffee for example causes irritability, impatience, tiredness, weakness and headaches. Fasting strips us down and exposes what we rely on for comfort, strength, relaxation and identity. Jesus encountered this same stripping down when he fasted from food forty days in the desert. But the story does not end with fasting. Jesus was also tested. Believers make a mistake when they view fasting as an end in itself. Fasting is a means of exposing what we rely on to a potentially idolatrous degree and preparing us for testing. A person who fasts from coffee may find their patience tested and lash out in anger. Coffee temporarily covered over their deep-seated anger. But fasting from coffee revealed something deeper God wants to crucify, so he can raise us to new life with Jesus.

Just as fasting is not an end in itself, neither is testing. The purpose of testing is to refine our faith in Jesus and bring forth our glorious new humanity. 1 Peter 1:6-7 affirms, "In this you greatly rejoice, even though now for a little while, if necessary, you have been distressed by various trials, that the proof of your faith, being

---

[16] I find the acronym ACELEP helpful to remember the 6 seasons of the Church Calendar: Advent, Christmas, Epiphany, Lent, Easter and Pentecost.

more precious than gold which is perishable, even though tested by fire, may be found to result in praise and glory and honor at the revelation of Jesus Christ." The testing of our faith is more precious than gold because testing prepares us for eternal life in Jesus' kingdom.

In the context of marriage counseling, God was stripping me of self-justification and dishonesty so he could test my love, humility and service toward my wife. The goal of this testing, whether I succeeded or failed, was to grow me as a new human in relationship to my wife.

Amazingly, Jesus was not only stripped down, tested and victorious in his wilderness temptation, he also encountered these realities on the cross. Soldiers literally stripped his clothes and exposed him to shame (John 19:23-24). The crowd, the thief and Jesus' own pain tested him with insults, challenges to come down, show his power and save himself (Matthew 27:40-46). In the face of each test, Jesus remained on the cross, prayed for his murderers and poured out his life for those he loved (Luke 23:24,43,46). He is the only human to remain sinless in the face of every test and respond in perfect love, even when people hated him. In Jesus' own words, "For them I sanctify myself, that they too may be truly sanctified" (John 17:19).

Third, God uses sanctification as a means of shaking our life to remove what is shakable and strengthen what is unshakable. Hebrews 12:28 says, "We are receiving a kingdom that cannot be shaken." Likewise 1 Corinthians 15:42-44,53-54 speaks of a resurrected body that is incorruptible, glorious, powerful, spiritually alive and immortal, in contrast to a non-resurrected earthly body that is corrupted, dishonored, weak, spiritually dead and mortal. This same theme of permanence and impermanence shows up again in Jesus' story of the house built on the rock. "When a flood came, the torrent struck that house but could not shake it, because it was well built" (Luke 6:48).

In each of these stories sin and disobedience leads to decay, death and destruction, while sanctification and the obedience of faith in God's word leads to new life, resurrection and permanence. To sin and disobey God is not just to be morally bad. To sin is to hasten our decay and shake the foundations of our house. Through the sanctifying rhythm of death and resurrection, God is testing and shaking our foundations in the current life. His goal is to strengthen us as new humans, prepared for Christ's return. In the words of Job, who also saw great testing, "When he has tested me, I will come forth as gold" (Job 23:10). Just as we have no need to fear life-experiences of death because of the inevitability of resurrection, we also have no need to fear the sanctifying death of our sin. Jesus is raising us to a holy and indestructible life.

Chapter 11: The Divine Facilitator

Resurrection Truth: The Holy Spirit applies Jesus' death and resurrection to make us new humans.

"The Spirit gives life." 2 Corinthians 3:6

Why is embracing the death and resurrection cycle so foreign and difficult for us humans? Through marriage counseling and reflection on the multi-level death occurring in our church and marriage, I discovered the greatest obstacle to dying and rising with Jesus is our self. Likewise, the greatest facilitator empowering and applying Jesus' death and resurrection in our life is the Holy Spirit. 1 Corinthians 2:12 confirms, "We have received...the Spirit who is from God, so that we may know the things freely given to us by God." One of the greatest gifts God has given us is the ability to rhythmically participate in Jesus' death and resurrection through our bodies.

Before we understand the Holy Spirit's role as facilitator of our participation in Jesus' death and resurrection, we first must understand the obstacle we pose. In one way or another we all try to be our own Messiah, create our own heaven on earth, make our own new humanity. We do this with the best of intentions. Instinctively from a young age we long for life not death, safety not vulnerability, goodness not evil, belonging not rejection, love not abuse. Inevitably we encounter something broken, something traumatic, some form of hell, rather than the heaven we desire. In response we viscerally recoil and labor to establish safety, peace, happiness and goodness in reaction to what threatens us. Being our own Messiah is our well-intentioned effort to create the elusive heaven we desire.

A young boy is neglected and ignored by absentee parents. He still longs for love, strength and family. When the pain of being rejected and ignored sets in, he determines never to be rejected or ignored again. He simultaneously insulates himself from people's rejection and acts out to ensure he won't be ignored. A young girl grows up with parents who are impossible to please. She falls short in countless ways, her parents remind her. The child still needs to be valued, affirmed and given purpose. Not receiving those foundations at home, she seeks her worth and purpose in other ways. A boyfriend, a job, perfectionism, addiction. Any of these outlets could offer a pseudo-heaven of acceptance and purpose, in place of her parent's impossible demands.

One heaven I tried to create in my marriage was peace, the absence of anger. As we saw in chapter 10, after an argument my wife would ask if I was okay. I wasn't, but out of emotional cowardice and self-protection I lied and said I was. Surely this was better than rocking the boat and getting stuck in a long tumultuous conversation. Other times my wife would get mad. I would shut down and freeze her out maintaining my cocoon of peace. I simply did not allow myself to express anger, disappointment or fear, though they still churned in my heart. I didn't want my wife to express these emotions either.

In retrospect I had meticulously eradicated significant ranges of emotions from my heart viewing them as a threat to my peace. When I encountered levels of anger, stress and ultimately professional and marital death beyond my ability to manage, attempts to be my own Messiah and create my own heaven quickly faltered. As it turns out, I am a clumsy, incompetent, brittle and ham-handed Messiah. My attempts to save myself fell apart under pressure. The sterile peace I had created for myself was an anemic imitation of the real peace heaven offers. Jesus' powerful new humanity, accomplished through his death and resurrection, presented a stark but hopeful contrast to my weak self-salvation.

But for Jesus to be our savior, healer and restorer, our attempts to create our own heaven and our own new humanity must step aside and die. After we die to saving our self, Jesus will raise us as new humans cared for and protected by the true savior, healer and creator. The person who applies Jesus' death and resurrection and makes our new humanity possible is the Holy Spirit.

Significantly theologians have described the Holy Spirit as the agent of creation.[17] The Spirit co-labors with Father and Son bringing all created things, visible and invisible, to fruition *ex nihilo*-- from nothing (Genesis 1:2, Hebrews 11:3). In Genesis 1 and John 1, the Father speaks the creative word, "Let there be" (Genesis 1:3). The Son proceeds as the Father's creative word made flesh, "and the Word became flesh" (John 1:14). The Holy Spirit implements and applies the will of Father and Son.

The Spirit shapes the universe (Genesis 1:2), supplies life to earthen Adam (Genesis 2:7), resurrects Israel after the death of exile (Ezekiel 37:14), enables the virgin Mary to conceive a child (Luke 1:35), anoints and empowers Jesus for ministry (Matthew 3:16), raises Jesus eternally from the dead (Romans 8:11), gives believers new birth (John 3:6), establishes the church at Pentecost (Acts 2:4) and empowers believers for new covenant faithfulness, in contrast to the powerlessness of the law (2 Corinthians 3:2-11).

With this history of bringing the divine word to life in creation, we should not be surprised to find the Holy Spirit at work again applying the creative power of Jesus' death and resurrection in the believer's life. Romans 8:13 affirms the Holy Spirit's work in

---

[17] I first heard this insight from John Frame, Systematic Theology Professor at Reformed Theological Seminary--Orlando, FL.

our death, "If by the Spirit you are putting to death the deeds of the body, you will live." Romans 8:11 points to the Spirit's work in our resurrection and new humanity, "But if the Spirit of Him who raised Jesus from the dead dwells in you, He who raised Christ Jesus from the dead will also give life to your mortal bodies through His Spirit who dwells in you." By his Spirit, God crucifies us with Christ, and by his Spirit he raises from the dead with Christ, not once but daily.

Practically, how does the Holy Spirit apply Jesus' death and resurrection to make us new humans? First we will examine what the Spirit crucifies in believers. Then we will examine what the Spirit raises to life. God's destruction of sin through Noah's flood and God's judgment of sin on the cross through Jesus provide a helpful illustration of the Spirit's beautiful work of crucifying sin. When God destroyed evil in the time of Noah, the entire world (except eight people, animals and an ark) perished in the flood. Evil was so bound up with the human heart that to destroy evil was to destroy humanity. Remarkably, since Pentecost the Holy Spirit is killing evil in the human heart without killing humans. Such is the nature and power of Jesus' death and resurrection applied by the Holy Spirit. We are simultaneously being crucified with Christ while also being made alive in Christ.

Ephesians 2:1-3 defines the three enemies of God and his people as the world (corporate spiritual opposition to God), the flesh (internal personal opposition to God; not physical flesh) and the devil. All three will be permanently and completely put to death when Jesus returns and reigns in the new heavens and new earth. Until then, the Holy Spirit progressively applies Jesus' death to believers, particularly in the crucifixion of our flesh. Paul writes, "For the flesh sets its desire against the Spirit, and the Spirit against the flesh; for these are in opposition to one another, so that you may not do the things that you please" and "Those who belong to Christ Jesus have crucified the flesh with its passions and desires" (Galatians 5:17,24).

In discussing crucifixion of the flesh (Greek: *sarx*), believers often miss the flesh's dual manifestations.[18] The deeds of the flesh (Galatians 5:19-21) read like a who's-who of infamous sins and tend to be more familiar. But two chapters earlier Paul warned, "Are you so foolish? Having begun by the Spirit, are you now being perfected by the flesh (Greek: *sarx*)?" (Galatians 3:3). In other words, two manifestations of the flesh oppose the Spirit's work of death and resurrection in believers.

The first manifestation consists of deeds such as sorcery, impurity, outbursts of anger and strife. The second manifestation consists of self-perfection, self-made goodness and self-directed religious effort to the exclusion of God's Spirit working in us. In other words, attempting to be our own Messiah. Galatians 3:3 indicates the Spirit began a death and resurrection work in the church at Galatia, but the flesh (internal personal opposition to God) crept in, took over and tried to perfect God's work through independent human effort. Galatians is perhaps Paul's most stark warning that self-perfection apart from faith in Christ and the work of the Holy Spirit is an impossibility, a fool's errand. Strikingly, the flesh has a good religious manifestation and a bad sinful manifestation. Paul rebukes both. The Spirit opposes both. All manifestations of the flesh must die. The Spirit of God creates the life of Christ in us.

Believers often praise successful men and women, without concern for the source of their apparent success--the Spirit or the flesh. From God's perspective, efforts to improve and perfect ourselves apart from the Spirit are just as egregious a manifestation

---

[18] I owe this insight to Dr. Jimmy Agan, a mentor and friend, in private conversation.

of the flesh as immoral rebellion against God. Personally, I seemed like an exceptionally peaceful person well into my 30s. Much of my peace came through fleshly exertion (and natural personality disposition), not the Spirit applying Jesus' death and resurrection to make me a new human. We must repent and die to the immoral deeds of the flesh and fleshly efforts to create our own new humanity, our own feeble heaven. The Spirit's record as agent of creation far surpasses any frail fleshly attempts to perfect what God began.

In addition to applying Jesus' death, the Holy Spirit also applies Jesus' resurrection to make us new humans. We saw in chapter 5 Jesus' resurrection inevitably swallows death. Similarly, the Spirit's work of resurrection in believers inevitably swallows and surpasses his crucifixion of our flesh. Crucifixion is God's appointed means to the end of resurrection, not an end in itself.

The Spirit's diversity of work in the first creation of Genesis 1 and 2 provides a helpful template for his diversity of work in the new creation of believers through Jesus. How many types of fruit, species of animals, diversity of galaxies and variations of cells did the Holy Spirit form in the first creation? If God's revelation of grace through Jesus Christ is greater than his revelation of grace in the Old Testament, shouldn't we expect the new creation work of the Holy Spirit through Jesus' death and resurrection to be greater than his first creation work?

Perhaps the best phrase for the Spirit's work of resurrection in believers is "escalation of life." The escalation of life occurs in at least 9 ways. He escalates holiness (2 Corinthians 7:1; Romans 12:1), character (Romans 5:3-5), intimacy with God (Hebrews 4:16), glory (2 Corinthians 3:18), power (2 Corinthians 4:7), family (1 Corinthians 12:12-14), inheritance (Ephesians 1:13-14), knowledge (Colossians 1:9) and fruitfulness (John 15:8). To illustrate the Spirit's escalation of life, we will trace the theme of fruitfulness

59

from Genesis to Revelation. If space permitted, we could demonstrate the same escalation through the Spirit's work in each theme above. Chapter 17 will return to the escalation of power and glory.

In the beginning God made the Garden of Eden fruitful, without inhibition (Genesis 1:11-12). After Adam and Eve ate the forbidden fruit, God inhibited fruitfulness by cursing the ground and giving Eve pain in child labor (Genesis 3:16-19). Inhibited fruitfulness continues throughout the Old Testament. Even with God's promise of blessing and fruitfulness in the promised land (Deuteronomy 30:9-10), Israel's fruitfulness falters, ending mired in the swamp of exile and a stalled restoration at the Old Testament's close. Jesus continues the theme of fruitfulness comparing his kingdom to abnormally fruitful seeds (Luke 8:4-15), a fruitful vine and branches (John 15:1-11) and a seed that dies in order to bear much fruit (John 12:23-25). Nearing the end of his earthly ministry, Jesus enters Jerusalem to cleanse the temple, but first curses the unfruitful fig tree, which failed to bear the fruit he expected (Mark 11:12-21).

Following Jesus' ascension, the apostles further develop the theme of escalating fruitfulness. Jesus is the first fruits of all who will be raised from the dead (1 Corinthians 15:20,23). Believers receive the Holy Spirit as the first fruit of our redemption (Romans 8:23). Early Christians are the first fruit of God's ongoing work in the world (2 Thessalonians 2:13; James 1:18). The Holy Spirit bears abundant fruit in Christ's followers (Galatians 5:22-23), and Paul sees an escalation of global fruitfulness. "The gospel is bearing fruit and growing throughout the whole world" (Colossians 1:6). Christ holds a sickle to harvest fruit from the earth at his return (Revelation 14:14-16). And finally the New Testament canon closes with a restored Eden and "the tree of life, bearing twelve crops of fruit, yielding its fruit every month" (Revelation 22:2). Blight, drought, famine and pestilence are no more. Prolific fruitfulness now abounds every month without inhibition.

Fruitfulness is one of many ways the Holy Spirit escalates life in believers by applying Jesus' death and resurrection. We could trace the Spirit's same work in many other areas. But only the Holy Spirit can give us the new humanity, the true heaven, the eternal escalation of life we desire. We cannot perfect ourselves from our own selfishness, pathology and pride. We cannot raise ourselves to our own glory, perfection and beauty. The Spirit led Jesus to the cross and raised him from the dead as a new human. Through repentance and faith in Jesus the Spirit will do the same in us.

As the illusion of being my own Messiah died and the reality of Jesus as a far superior Messiah grew, my marriage began to change. I was less scared to be honest when my wife asked how I was doing. I spent less time running away and protecting myself from my wife's emotions. I grew in emotional courage and pursued my wife more diligently, even when the pursuit was emotionally difficult. The power of the Holy Spirit to apply Jesus' Messianic way of death and resurrection to my life made all the difference. Acting as my own Messiah, I was incapable of raising dead emotions or situations to life. I simply fought to maintain the minimalistic and one-dimensional picture of a peaceful heaven I could envision. But with Jesus as my Messiah and my body enlivened by his Spirit, I could face danger, death, embrace pain and engage my fears with complete confidence that after I died with Jesus, the same Spirit that raised Christ from the dead would also raise me from the dead.

Chapter 12: What About Jesus' Teachings?

Resurrection Truth: Jesus' teaching models a lifestyle of death and resurrection.

"Blessed are those who mourn, for they will be comforted."
Matthew 5:4

Thus far the cycle of death and resurrection has provided a compelling framework for how we become new humans, grow in sanctification and deal with severe loss and disappointment. But how do death and resurrection relate to other aspects of daily life such as driving to work, taking out the trash, being married and growing old? Often more challenging than dying and rising with Jesus in traumatic life situations, as Paul describes in 2 Corinthians 4:10, is daily dying and rising with Jesus in obedience to his teachings. Far from being stand-alone miraculous events with no relevance to his teaching, death and resurrection permeate Jesus' teaching. We could summarize Jesus' teaching as calling forth a death and resurrection lifestyle. Jesus not only died and rose to create a new human race. By his teaching, he gave new humans a death and resurrection blueprint for life. Practically, how do we live as new humans and follow Jesus' teachings in a world of violent crime, long-term unemployment, family dysfunction and societal division?

First, Jesus calls us to repent and believe the gospel following the pattern of death and resurrection. Especially when combined with John the Baptist's ministry of baptizing Jews, a practice associated with gentile conversion to Judaism, the call to repentance is particularly revolutionary. In essence John and Jesus are calling people who consider themselves God's chosen people and children of Abraham to die to their biological identity, religious pedigree and sin. In turn Jesus will raise those who repent and are baptized to new life in his kingdom. Jesus proclaims, "The time has come. The kingdom of God has come near. Repent and believe the good news" (Mark 1:15). This call to repentance continues through Jesus' ministry and into Peter's sermon at Pentecost (Acts 2:38). Death and resurrection through repentance and faith begins and continues Jesus' new humanity ministry to this day.

Second, in one of his most famous teachings Jesus redefines the happy or blessed life around the pattern of his death and resurrection. In Matthew 5:3-12, commonly called "the beatitudes," Jesus describes the blessed life as follows:

> [3]Blessed are the poor in spirit, for theirs is the kingdom of heaven.
> [4] Blessed are those who mourn, for they will be comforted.
> [5] Blessed are the meek, for they will inherit the earth.
> [6] Blessed are those who hunger and thirst for righteousness, for they will be filled.
> [7] Blessed are the merciful, for they will be shown mercy.
> [8] Blessed are the pure in heart, for they will see God.
> [9] Blessed are the peacemakers, for they will be called children of God.
> [10] Blessed are those who are persecuted because of righteousness, for theirs is the kingdom of heaven.
> [11] "Blessed are you when people insult you, persecute you and falsely say all kinds of evil against you because of me. [12] Rejoice and be glad, because great is your reward in heaven, for in the same way they persecuted the prophets who were before you.

Numerous beatitudes echo the pattern of death and resurrection. For example the "poor in spirit" of verse 3 represent dependency, weakness and lowliness, yet they are exalted with life in the kingdom of heaven. The "pure in heart" of verse 8 closely resemble those who have died to sin, yet they are raised to life with the promise "they will see God."

One of the strongest connections to death and resurrection comes in verse 4, "Blessed are those who mourn, for they will be comforted." What is mourning, except a response to various forms of death? Yet Jesus promises that those who recognize death and mourn its effects will be comforted. The Greek word for comfort in Matthew 5:4 is *paraklethesontai*. John 14:16 uses a form of the same Greek word (*parakleton*) to describe the coming Holy Spirit, "the Comforter," whom the Father will send believers after Jesus' resurrection from the dead and ascension to heaven. Finally, Revelation 21:4 describes a picture of ultimate comfort after Jesus returns and the dead are raised. "He will wipe every tear from their eyes. There will be no more death or mourning or crying or pain, for the old order of things has passed away." From the Beatitudes to the book of Revelation, Jesus calls his followers to embrace death and resurrection through mourning, poverty in spirit and purity of heart. In turn God will comfort and resurrect them, pour out his Spirit and bring them to his heavenly kingdom.

Third, Jesus reframes the ethical life using themes of death and resurrection. In the Sermon on the Mount from Matthew 5:1-7:29, Jesus increases the standards for holiness, justice, love, piety and faith. Regarding holiness, Jesus calls for a higher standard than merely avoiding physical adultery. The person who looks at a woman lustfully has committed adultery in his heart. Jesus prescribes cutting off and killing the source of sin because, "It is better for you to lose one part of your body than for your whole body to go into hell" (Matthew 5:30).[19] Death to sin and

---

[19] Matthew 18:8-9 repeats and elaborates on Matthew 5:30 making the ethical

resurrection to life are better than embracing sin and suffering the death of hell.

For Jesus justice no longer means retaliating "eye for eye, and tooth for tooth" (Matthew 5:38) when we suffer injustice. Love no longer means, "Love your neighbor and hate your enemy" (Matthew 5:43). Rather, Jesus redefines justice as suffering wrong, showing grace to our oppressor and practicing non-retaliation when beaten. Each of these responses require the death of our desire for exacting our own justice, just as Jesus responded with longsuffering and mercy to those who threatened, mocked and schemed against him. Likewise Jesus now defines love as follows, "Love your enemies and pray for those who persecute you" (Matthew 5:44). Luke 6:27-28 adds, "Love your enemies, do good to those who hate you, bless those who curse you, pray for those who mistreat you." Jesus explains the motivation for this form of love in Matthew 5:45-48:

> Be children of your Father in heaven. He causes his sun to rise on the evil and the good, and sends rain on the righteous and the unrighteous. If you love those who love you, what reward will you get? Are not even the tax collectors doing that? And if you greet only your own people, what are you doing more than others? Do not even pagans do that? Be perfect, therefore, as your heavenly Father is perfect.

---

connection between death to sin and inheritance of new life even more explicit. "If your hand or your foot causes you to stumble, cut it off and throw it from you; it is better for you to enter life crippled or lame, than to have two hands or two feet and be cast into the eternal fire. If your eye causes you to stumble, pluck it out and throw it from you. It is better for you to enter life with one eye, than to have two eyes and be cast into the fiery hell."

Once again, death and resurrection are at work. We die to our definition of love which only loves when it receives love in return. We give up our desire to nurse grudges, punish our enemy and withhold good from our detractors. Instead we emulate our Heavenly Father who extends sacrificial love even to his enemies (Romans 5:8).

Fourth, Jesus' parables repeatedly commend and foreshadow the realities of death and resurrection. The parable of the dinner guests in Luke 14:7-15 encourages participants to take a seat of lower honor at the banquet table with the chance of being invited to a seat of greater honor. Jesus reasons, "Everyone who exalts himself will be humbled, and he who humbles himself will be exalted" (Luke 14:11). Throughout the New Testament, humiliation and exaltation are regular synonyms for death and resurrection.

At the same banquet, Jesus instructs the host not to invite friends, family and rich neighbors, who will likely repay the host in the future. Instead Jesus instructs, "When you give a reception, invite the poor, the crippled, the lame, the blind, and you will be blessed, since they do not have the means to repay you; for you will be repaid at the resurrection of the righteous" (Luke 14:13-14). Once again extending kindness to the disadvantaged, dying to the expectation of earthly repayment and looking to the resurrection of the righteous forms the basis for Jesus' new human lifestyle in the present. We've also seen death and resurrection serve as a synonym for rebellion and repentance in the parable of the prodigal son. The joyful father celebrates because "This son of mine was dead and has come to life again; he was lost and has been found.' And they began to celebrate" (Luke 15:24).

Fifth, Jesus' actions model a lifestyle of death and resurrection. Jesus welcomed his own baptism, an image of death and resurrection (Matthew 3:13-17). At his trial Jesus literally turned the other cheek in accord with his own teaching. When slapped he refused to retaliate (John 18:23-24). Instead of retaliation, Jesus embraced unjust death and entrusted himself to his Father for justice. This justice would come through his resurrection from the dead. In the words of Peter, "While being reviled, He did not revile in return; while suffering, He uttered no threats, but kept entrusting Himself to Him who judges righteously" (1 Peter 2:22-23). Before his crucifixion Jesus acted as a servant and washed his disciples feet, foreshadowing his humble death and his sacrifice for the sins of the world (John 13:5-20). In Philippians 2:5-11, Paul views the entirety of Jesus' life as prescriptive for the attitude the Philippians should have in themselves:

> Have this attitude in yourselves which was also in Christ Jesus, 6 who, although He existed in the form of God, did not regard equality with God a thing to be grasped, 7 but emptied Himself, taking the form of a bond-servant, and being made in the likeness of men. 8 Being found in appearance as a man, He humbled Himself by becoming obedient to the point of death, even death on a cross. 9 For this reason also, God highly exalted Him, and bestowed on Him the name which is above every name, 10 so that at the name of Jesus EVERY KNEE WILL BOW, of those who are in heaven and on earth and under the earth, 11 and that every tongue will confess that Jesus Christ is Lord, to the glory of God the Father.

Even Jesus' incarnation foreshadowed rejection and death as Herod sought to extinguish Jesus' young life, "Then when Herod saw that he had been tricked by the magi, he became very enraged, and sent and slew all the male children who were in Bethlehem and all its vicinity, from two years old and under, according to the time which he had determined from the magi" (Matthew 2:16).

Each of these actions represent a tremendous humiliation and giving up of rights. The Maker of lips allowed himself to be spit upon. The judge of the universe allowed himself to be falsely judged. The Lord of all made himself servant of all. The Giver of life allowed his life to be taken. The One worthy of all worship presented himself for mocking. In fact, Jesus' teachings, actions and parables make no sense apart from the framework of death and resurrection. Without resurrection, Jesus becomes a mere sadist, a kamikaze pilot, someone who suffers for suffering's sake. With resurrection, Jesus creates new humans who follow his death and resurrection lifestyle and teaching.

How do we follow Jesus and his apostle's teachings as new humans in the present? Several examples from daily life will help illustrate this reality. When we are cut off in traffic, we are not just furious drivers. We are new humans learning how to "forgive one another, just as God in Christ forgave [us]" (Ephesians 4:28). When we get married, we are not just making ourselves happy. We are new humans living out the words of Christ who said, "Love one another as I have loved you" (John 13:34). When we clean toilets or take out trash, we are not just doing dirty work. We are new humans walking in the footsteps of Jesus who "did not come to be served, but to serve" (Matthew 20:28). When we grow old, we are not just another day closer to death. We are new humans "being transformed into [Jesus'] image with ever increasing glory" (2 Corinthians 3:18). Jesus does not intend death and resurrection to only give us hope during difficult life moments. He also intends death and resurrection to shape us at all times, in all places. We are a death and resurrection people following the death and resurrection lifestyle of our death and resurrection Savior.

Chapter 13: Strength for the Journey

Resurrection Truth: Sacraments connect us with Jesus' death and resurrection to strengthen our new humanity.

"We have been buried with Him through baptism into death, so that as Christ was raised from the dead through the glory of the Father, so we too might walk in newness of life." Romans 6:4

"As often as you eat this bread and drink the cup, you proclaim the Lord's death until He comes." 1 Corinthians 11:26

If any doubt remained about the centrality of Jesus' death and resurrection for the life of new humans, Jesus' institution of baptism and communion should erase all uncertainty. Ritual reenactments of Jesus' death and resurrection are at the center of Christian worship. We enter the body of Christ--the church--through dying and rising with Jesus in baptism. God grows and feeds his people through communion, which visually depicts Jesus' death and resurrection.

In explaining the offensive symbol of the cross at the time of Jesus' earthly ministry, some have reasoned that wearing a gold cross in Jesus' day would be equivalent to wearing a gold electric chair or gold gallows as jewelry today. Gallows and electric chairs are prominent means of execution in modern history, just as the cross was a prominent Roman instrument of execution in Jesus' day. The analogy is compelling but incomplete. To be a Christian is not only to embrace the horrific symbol of the cross as an instrument of salvation. To be a Christian is to regularly reenact a ritual of crucifixion in the communion service and to rejoice in that execution and Jesus' subsequent resurrection from the dead. The equivalent today would be to regularly reenact a ritual of hanging or lethal injection followed by resurrection as a central joyful act of Christian public worship. In other words, ongoing participation in Jesus' death and resurrection is unavoidably central and foundational to the life of the church corporately gathered and individually dispersed.

As NT Wright has observed, embracing or destroying a symbol can evoke powerful cultural reactions.[20] We may be able to intellectualize, spiritualize or sanitize Jesus' words about death and resurrection. But participating in the symbols of bread (crucified body), wine (spilled blood) and water (burial by drowning and resurrection to new life), makes the reality of our death and resurrection with Jesus harder to ignore. To discern the role baptism and communion play in our life, we need to understand Jesus' institution of these sacraments, our ongoing participation in them and the implications of baptism and communion for the church.

Jesus instituted communion in the context of a Passover meal. Historically Passover celebrates God's liberation of his people from slavery in Egypt, his inauguration of a new nation journeying toward the promised land and God's provision of a sacrifice to preserve his people from death.[21] Jesus reinterprets the Passover in the context of his own death, resurrection and coming kingdom. The unleavened Passover bread is now Jesus' body which is broken and given for his people (Luke 22:19). The Passover cup is now Jesus' poured out blood of the new covenant (Luke 22:20).

God's covenant at Mount Sinai through Moses formed a nation. God's new covenant, prophesied in Jeremiah 31:27-34,

---

[20] Wright, *Jesus and the Victory of God*, 369-442. Wright addresses an entire chapter to symbols entitled, "Symbols and Controversy."
[21] According to Exodus 12:1-2, Passover also marks the new beginning of Israel's calendar, just as Jesus' death and resurrection marks the new beginning of God's redemptive work through the church.

through Jesus' body and blood establishes a new people and a new nation who will never die or be overthrown. Jesus calls his new people, forged by his death and resurrection, to celebrate the new Passover meal "in remembrance of me" (Luke 22:19). Jesus himself will not eat the meal again until he comes again in his kingdom. Communion therefore looks back to Jesus' crucifixion and forward to his return when he raises the dead and consummates his eternal unopposed kingdom.[22]

Jesus' institution of baptism as the basis for entrance into his church also makes his death and resurrection unavoidably central to his new covenant community. In Matthew 3:13-17 Jesus begins his ministry receiving John's baptism of repentance for the forgiveness of sins. In Mark 10:37-40 Jesus contrasts James and John's desire for the glory of sitting on Jesus' right and left hand to the baptism of a humiliating death and a triumphant resurrection Jesus must undergo. Finally Jesus concludes his earthly ministry in Matthew 28:16-20 commanding all his future followers to be baptized and taught his words. During the start, continuation and conclusion of Jesus' earthly ministry baptism foreshadows and remembers Jesus' death and resurrection.

Jesus prophecies the centrality of his own death and resurrection three times en route to Jerusalem (Mark 8:31-33; 9:30-32; 10:33-34). To these prophecies and the final events of Jesus' life, Jesus adds baptism and communion as tangible rituals of participation in his death and resurrection. Jesus' institution of

---

[22] Christian worship traditions that celebrate communion less frequently will have a harder time relating to the centrality of death and resurrection in communion. Traditions who celebrate communion weekly are more likely to be tangibly formed by the rhythm of death and resurrection with Jesus. From Justin Martyr's description of early Christian worship in his *First Apology* and from Acts 20:7 where Paul celebrates communion "on the first day of the week," I believe the early church celebrated communion weekly.

these rites looks beyond his own death and resurrection to an ongoing implementation of that life in his followers.

After Jesus' ascension in glory to reign at his Father's right hand, his followers continued the acts of baptism and communion Jesus instituted. The early Church viewed themselves as ongoing participants in Jesus' death and resurrection. They also viewed baptism and communion with Jesus as the means by which they became new humans and received ongoing nourishment in the new human life.

Paul asks the Corinthians rhetorically, "Is not the cup of blessing which we bless a sharing in the blood of Christ? Is not the bread which we break a sharing in the body of Christ?" (1 Corinthians 10:16). The Greek word *koinonia* is variously translated "communion," "sharing in," "fellowship" or "participation in." Paul regarded the Corinthian church's participation in Jesus' body and blood through the breaking of bread and the sharing of the cup as a source of either blessing or judgment for the church, depending on the Corinthian's repentance and faith toward God. Communion received without repentance could make the Corinthians sick or even subject to premature death (1 Corinthians 11:30). Communion received in repentance and faith was a source of blessing (1 Corinthians 10:16), unity (1 Corinthians 10:17) and spiritual food (1 Corinthians 10:3).

Likewise, Paul taught the Romans they were participating in Jesus' crucifixion of their old self and resurrection to new life through baptism. Romans 6:3-9 states:

> 3 Do you not know that all of us who have been baptized into Christ Jesus have been baptized into His death?
> 4 Therefore we have been buried with Him through baptism into death, so that as Christ was raised from the dead through the glory of the Father, so we too might walk

in newness of life.[5] For if we have become united with Him in the likeness of His death, certainly we shall also be in the likeness of His resurrection,[6] knowing this, that our old self was crucified with Him, in order that our body of sin might be done away with, so that we would no longer be slaves to sin; [7] for he who has died is freed from sin. [8] Now if we have died with Christ, we believe that we shall also live with Him,[9] knowing that Christ, having been raised from the dead, is never to die again; death no longer is master over Him.

Other benefits of participating in Jesus' death and resurrection through baptism include the circumcision of our sinful nature by Christ (Colossians 2:11), salvation from judgment (1 Peter 3:21), forgiveness of our sins (Acts 2:38), reception of the Holy Spirit (Acts 2:38) and unity as one body (1 Corinthians 12:13). As we have seen in previous chapters, the crucifixion of the sinful nature, filling with the Holy Spirit and resurrection with Jesus are the means by which God makes us new humans. Baptism and communion are the temporal tangible events Jesus uses to represent and accomplish the new human life in all who turn to him in repentance and faith.

Beyond participating in Jesus' death and resurrection as new humans, the New Testament also views baptism and communion as a strong basis for corporate and individual ethics in the church. According to Paul, people who experience Jesus' death and resurrection through baptism and communion should think and act in a manner consistent with these practices Jesus commanded. Corporately, the Corinthian church should not selfishly get drunk and gorge themselves during communion while their more impoverished brothers and sisters in Christ go hungry (1 Corinthians 11:20-22). The church at Corinth should also cease its division and boasting in Paul, Apollos and Cephas. None of these men were crucified for the Corinthians or serve as the basis for the

Corinthian's baptism (1 Corinthians 1:12-13). Selfishness, drunkenness, carelessness toward the poor and division are all inconsistent with the new human life Jesus desired to live out corporately in his people through baptism and communion.

Last, baptism and communion shape the individual ethics of Jesus' followers. Paul sees the washing of Jesus' followers and union with Christ in baptism as the basis for fleeing sexual immorality (1 Corinthians 6:11-20). Likewise, communion with Christ through bread and wine forms the basis for fleeing idolatry (1 Corinthians 10:14-22). Whether corporately or individually baptism and communion serve as concrete reference points connecting believers to Jesus' death and resurrection while also shaping the ethics of their new humanity.

Part 3: Death, Resurrection and Mission

Chapter 14: Do Yin and Yang = Death and Resurrection?

Resurrection Truth: Other religions incorporate cyclical beliefs, but the death and resurrection cycle of Christianity is unique.

"I am the Alpha and the Omega, the first and the last, the beginning and the end." Revelation 22:12-13

In Part 1 we examined how Jesus applies the cycle of death and resurrection in the life of his individual followers. In Part 2 we explored the role of Jesus' death and resurrection in forming a new humanity who will live, rule and worship eternally in God's new heavens and new earth. In Part 3 we will survey world view implications of Jesus' rhythmic death and resurrection in the life of his people.

Hinduism and Buddhism have the cycle of samsara shaped by personal desire and karma. Taoism and Confucianism have the continuous interplay of yin and yang. Judaism has the rhythm of creation, exile, deliverance and restoration. Christians have the cycle of dying and rising with Jesus. These religions are not equivalent in message or meaning. But they do each possess cycles or rhythms that claim to make sense of the universe and shape the behavior of their adherents. How is the Christian cycle of death and resurrection with Jesus unique, and what similarities or differences does Christianity have with other religions?

Hinduism and Buddhism view earthly existence as a continues cycle of life, death and reincarnation. This cycle, called samsara, is characterized by suffering and shaped by one's actions and desires. The goal of life in Buddhism is to escape the cycle of samsara by ceasing personal desire, meditating on the Eight Noble

Truths and entering nirvana, where re-death and re-birth are no more. Similarly in Hinduism, from which Buddhism originated, one escapes samsara through good personal karma (actions), resulting in the permanent reunification of the soul or self with Brahman (eternal unchanging reality beyond the current world).

What similarities and differences exist between these two eastern religions and Christianity? First, all three religions recognize and teach the cyclical nature of life. Second, each religion also addresses the question of human suffering and the ultimate goal of human existence. Third, these religions all advocate the refinement of personal character through a cyclical process. Beyond these similarities, many differences also exist.

First, the cycle of death and resurrection in Christianity is focused within the present earthly life of the individual and ends with physical death. Christianity does not teach the transmigration of the individual soul through repeated earthly lives, so the cycle of death and resurrection does not continue beyond the present life, as in Hinduism and Buddhism. Second, Christianity takes a more positive view of suffering, often viewing suffering as a source of power, sanctification and blessing in believer's lives. The ultimate goal of Christianity is not to escape the cycle of suffering, but rather to embrace suffering, die and rise with Jesus and thereby enter his glory. Third Father, Son and Holy Spirit personally direct the cycle of death and resurrection in Christianity, after the pattern of Jesus' own death and resurrection. In Christianity God, in the person of Jesus Christ, suffers with us, tasting death and resurrection himself. Fourth, Jesus' death and resurrection as God in flesh presume our human inability to escape death, sin and brokenness apart from divine intervention. Fifth, the eschatological goal of Christian death and resurrection is personal resurrected bodily life in a renewed physical universe. Christian believers will receive individual rewards, judgment and personal responsibilities in the life to come.

We will see and know Jesus face to face in an eternally heightened state of love, joy, knowledge, life and peace.

How does Christianity compare to the Taoist and Confucian rhythms of yin-yang interplay found in ancient Chinese philosophy? According to Taoism and Confucianism yin and yang form opposites such as dark and light, male and female, hot and cold. These opposites simultaneously compliment and form tension with each other. If yin and yang lose balance in people or the cosmos, disruption follows. By striving toward equilibrium, yin and yang create life and energy in the universe.

Once again, Christianity holds similarities and differences with the yin-yang rhythmic interplay of Taoism and Confucianism. Like yin-yang, Christianity recognizes opposites such as light and dark, death and resurrection, dry land and sea. Christianity also teaches the importance of balance and harmony in the created universe. The blotting out of the sun by darkness as in Isaiah 13:10 or the usurping of dry land by water as in the story of Noah's flood typically results in the destruction of the created order. In response to the flood of Noah's day, God promises to preserve the balance of created life in Genesis 8:22, "While the earth remains, seedtime and harvest, and cold and heat, and summer and winter, and day and night shall not cease."

Besides these similarities, Christianity also holds great differences with Taoism and Confucianism's yin-yang interplay. Jesus' permanent resurrection from the dead has unveiled an eternal destiny that will alter the balance of yin and yang. For example, when Christ returns and raises the dead, he will establish a kingdom in which there will be no more night. As Revelation 22:5 describes, "There will no longer be any night; and they will not have need of the light of a lamp nor the light of the sun, because the Lord God will illumine them; and they will reign forever and ever." Likewise, according to Revelation 21:1 the sea will also one day be abolished. "Then I saw a new heaven and a new earth; for the first heaven and the first earth passed away, and there is no longer any sea." Even if the passing away of night and sea are interpreted metaphorically, the contrast with yin-yang's philosophy of balance between dark and light still remains.

Even with male and female, Jesus predicts a time when "in the resurrection they neither marry nor are given in marriage" (Matthew 22:30). The current realities of male and female marital relationship will change at the time of resurrection. Jesus' death and resurrection sets Christianity apart from every other world religion by pointing to a future reality beyond what our physical eyes currently observe. Christianity points to a time when death and sin will be abolished, a new heavens and new earth will descend and all opposition to Jesus' authority will be abolished. When Hinduism, Buddhism, Taoism, Confucianism and Christianity make observations about the material world and life experience common to all humanity, such as suffering, life and death, these religions hold several threads in common. In matters related to Jesus' death, resurrection and the implications of these events for humanity and the universe, Christianity diverges significantly. According to the New Testament Jesus' death and resurrection reveal a higher culminating reality than humans are able to discover through independent observation of the universe.

Not surprisingly, the cyclical realities of Judaism and Christianity hold the most in common. The Jewish Bible (which Christians call the Old Testament) depicts a reoccurring cycle of creation, exile, deliverance and restoration. In Genesis 1 and 2, God creates the heavens and the earth. Adam and Eve succumb to temptation and face exile from the Garden of Eden. Yet God clothes Adam and Eve, promising them ultimate deliverance and victory over the serpent through a "seed" of the woman in Genesis 3:15. "And I will put enmity between you and the woman, and between your seed and her seed; he shall strike you on the head, and you shall strike him on the heel."

After Israel grew they again found themselves enslaved as exiles in Egypt. God raised up a deliverer, Moses, who led Israel out of slavery toward a new promised land. Before he died and before Israel entered the promised land, Moses predicted in Deuteronomy 4:25-31 that Israel would face exile and again need restoration by the hand of the Lord. The book of Judges contains repeated cycles of moral rebellion against God, enslavement by a foreign power, repentance, and deliverance from the oppressive foreign power. Last, during Israel and Judah's Assyrian, Babylonian and Persian exiles, prophets such as Isaiah, Jeremiah and Ezekiel look forward to a time of deliverance when God will bring forth a new creation, new exodus, new covenant and new temple.

Where do Christianity and Judaism differ in their cyclical conceptions of reality? First, Christianity has adopted and expanded the Genesis teaching that all people are in exile from the life of God due to sin and death. Paul now views Jesus as the new Adam who has come to deliver and restore God's people and creation from Adam's original exile. "For as in Adam all die, so also in Christ all will be made alive" (1 Corinthians 15:22). The New Testament sees Jesus entering exile with and for his people, so he can lead them out of exile by his resurrection from the dead. Hebrews 13:11-14 states:

> [11] For the bodies of those animals whose blood is brought into the holy place by the high priest as an offering for sin, are burned outside the camp. [12] Therefore Jesus also, that He might sanctify the people through His own blood, suffered outside the gate. [13] So, let us go out to Him outside the camp, bearing His reproach. [14] For here we do not have a lasting city, but we are seeking the city which is to come.

Second, by participating in Jesus' death and resurrection through faith, Christianity extends the imagery of exile, deliverance and restoration to all people, both Jews and Gentiles. In short Jesus completes the exile-deliverance-restoration cycle by his own death, resurrection and the ascending embrace of his new humanity into the arms of heaven. As we embrace Jesus, heaven embraces us (Ephesians 2:6).

NT Wright's observation about the completion of Israel's grand cosmic narrative through the revelation of Jesus' death and resurrection holds true for other religions as well:

> For Paul, the narrative of scripture--the whole great sweep, from Genesis to 2 Chronicles...had found its spectacular resolution. Like the book of Acts for a first-time reader today, the Jewish scriptures stopped just too soon. The reader wants to know what happened to the hero, in this case, to Israel, and (so to speak) to God as well. Does the hero triumph? Will adversity, so long drawn out, finally be overcome? Yes, answers Paul: we have had a fresh apokalypsis, the unveiling of long-hidden mysteries, the discerning of age-old wisdom...As we know from his own retelling of the great narratives upon which he had previously lived in hope, not least that of the closing chapters of Deuteronomy, Paul was able now to tell the same story but...with the crucified and risen Jesus as its climax and its radical redefinition.[23]

In Jesus' death, resurrection and ascension, God revealed "something that had already happened as the answer to age-old

---

[23] Wright, *Paul and the Faithfulness of God*, 416.

prayers and wrestlings of prophets, sages and seers."[24] In other words God has made known how all stories and all cycles end. We are no longer blindly groping through suffering, failure and loss. We are carried along by the Holy Spirit as participants in Jesus' death and resurrection until we reach his current reality and our intended destiny, the tangible perfection and recreation of all things. Examining the cycles of various religions through the lens of Jesus' death, resurrection and ascension provides a helpful bridge for inter-religious dialogue and clear differentiation from other religious cycles.

_____

[24] Ibid., 416.

Chapter 15: A Gospel of Resurrection

Resurrection Truth: Death and resurrection shape our proclamation of the gospel.

"Be faithful until death, and I will give you the crown of life."
Revelation 2:10

What is the gospel, the good news of Jesus Christ (Mark 1:14)? How do Jesus' death and resurrection impact our proclamation of the gospel? Should we expect temporal earthly prosperity now and eternal prosperity later? Should we expect suffering now and hope for justice and relief later?

Death and resurrection provide a helpful framework for understanding and proclaiming the gospel. Christian individuals or traditions that downplay either Jesus' death or resurrection in their theology do a disservice to themselves and experience a truncated gospel. Consider five gospel emphases rooted in a strong theology of Jesus' death and resurrection.

First, Jesus' death and resurrection should embolden our proclamation of God's salvation to all who are hurting, broken or walking in darkness. If Jesus has made death (both his and ours) a necessary and even mandatory forerunner to resurrection, we should not be surprised, hopeless or fearful when we encounter death in various forms. A child is rebelliously careening off our desired ethical path for their life. A marriage is experiencing slow motion collapse. An act of racism is tearing a community apart. Spiritual influences of addiction, greed and hatred are degrading a nation. Each of these realities, though heartbreaking, express what we already know. Death is a pervasive and inescapable reality of the world in which we live. What the unbelieving world does not yet know is that when we recognize death and turn to the giver of life, Jesus is faithful to raise the dead. With Jesus, life swallows death. Death does not swallow life.

Mark's account of the Gerasene demoniac (Mark 5:1-20) offers a helpful perspective through which to view Jesus' engagement with brokenness and darkness. A man who lived in the country of the Gerasenes was possessed by a legion of demons. He lived among the tombs, possessed superhuman strength, cut himself with rocks and screamed night and day. Townspeople tried to bind him with chains and shackles, but the demon possessed man broke all physical bonds.

The story evokes images of self-harm, madness, degraded humanity and alienation from society. Townspeople may have noticed the man's condition deteriorating--deeper cuts, louder screams, more superhuman strength. (Such an unwelcome guest surely didn't help local tourism and business traffic.) The Gerasenes' coping strategy for this demon possessed madman settled on containment. They couldn't do anything about his demons or degraded humanity. Chaining him would have to do. But even that failed.

When Jesus came on the scene, he met the man in the open. Jesus recognized and addressed the man's true condition without fear. He spoke first to the man's demons, casting them out, and then to the man himself. Following the demon's exorcism into two thousand pigs, townspeople streamed to witness the formerly demon possessed man. He was sitting, clothed and in his right mind. Jesus had restored his humanity, which the legion of demons destroyed. The new man wanted to follow Jesus, but Jesus sent him home to proclaim the Lord's deeds and power.

Today we often witness similar personal, cultural or familial deterioration. Like the Gerasene townspeople, we fret, make attempts to contain the situation and seek to insulate ourselves from its impact. Yet this is not how Jesus addressed death, bondage and decay. He addressed the powers of bondage, broke their control and restored the demoniac to peaceful humanity.[25] Upon the liberated man's return home, we can imagine his parents rejoicing along with the prodigal son's father. "This son of mine was dead and has come to life again; he was lost and has been found" (Luke 15:24). Stories of individual or cultural degradation may strike us with fear or panic. But people who know the power of Jesus' death and resurrection should not be surprised by death or stop laboring for resurrection. Life swallows death.

Second, a robust emphasis on death and resurrection will increase the gospel's engagement with culture and society. NT Wright has observed that "orthodox Christianity has found it hard to respond to the attacks of secular modernity" partially because we have preferred a theology of 'going to heaven' (implicitly escaping earth) over a theology of resurrection into new humanity and a renewed creation.[26] What do the contemporary phrases "making the world a better place," "making a difference" and "being the change you want to see in the world" represent but cries for a new world and a new humanity? If people unknowingly seek what Jesus is building, isn't new humanity at least a starting point for conversation between Christians and secularists. New humanity also offers an unexpected and compelling way to proclaim the gospel within contemporary western culture that is very concerned about societal justice.

I have coined the following axiom as a helpful way of understanding a dual thrust of Jesus' salvation. "Through his death and resurrection, Jesus makes the bad things right and the good things better." Christians tend to focus on how Jesus' death makes

---

[25] I first heard this insight about evil degrading humanity and Jesus restoring humanity from Dr. Allen Mawhinney, a former New Testament professor at Reformed Theological Seminary-Orlando.
[26] NT Wright, *Resurrection of the Son of God*, 368.

the bad things right. It is true sin does need to be cleansed and forgiven. Wickedness does need to be judged. Rebellion does need to be overthrown. Christ dealt a fatal blow to sin and evil on the cross and will permanently abolish them at his return. But a gospel focused only on bad things being made right is a remedial and incomplete gospel. Believers who focus primarily on suffering, evil and Jesus' death are familiar with themes of hardship, sorrow and unworthiness. But themes of victory, joy and glory embodied in Jesus' resurrection remain more foreign and need greater exploration.

What does it mean for Jesus to be making the good things better through his resurrection? Before Jesus came, God gave good gifts such as birth, creation, commandments, covenants, Jerusalem and the human heart. As good as these gifts are, God is making them better. Through Jesus' death and resurrection, he is establishing a new birth (1 Peter 1:3), new creation (2 Corinthians 5:17), new commandment (John 13:34), new covenant (Luke 22:20), new Jerusalem (Revelation 21:2) and new heart (Ezekiel 36:26). In the words of Revelation 21:5 spoken from the heavenly throne, "Behold, I am making all things new" (Revelation 21:5). What seems good to us is preliminary and incomplete to God. He is making the good things better. While the gospel does bring remediation for sinners, it also presents a progressive redemptive vision to make what is good even better.

Consider a familiar conversation between believers and non-believers. A non-believer considers them self a good person. The believer, knowing Jesus died for sinners, attempts to convince the non-believer they are sinful and need a Savior. The non-believer gets offended, considers the believer a self-righteous prude and regards the gospel as a message about hell, judgment and hate.

Jesus and his apostles present the gospel in different ways to different audiences, while never denying the clear truths of the gospel. In the scenario above, what if the believer, instead of trying to convince the non-believer they are bad, explained all the ways Jesus is progressively making good things better and eventually perfect? Would this not be a compelling and disarming way to present the gospel impact of Jesus' death and resurrection?

Third, a robust theology of death and resurrection will increase dependency on God. Even before Jesus' death and resurrection, he and the Old Testament taught our total dependency on God for human life. In Matthew 6:28-30, Jesus compares God's sustaining care for lilies to his even greater care for us:

> Observe how the lilies of the field grow; they do not toil nor do they spin, [29] yet I say to you that not even Solomon in all his glory clothed himself like one of these. [30] But if God so clothes the grass of the field, which is alive today and tomorrow is thrown into the furnace, will He not much more clothe you? You of little faith.

Likewise Psalm 123:2 proclaims, "Behold, as the eyes of servants look to the hand of their master, as the eyes of a maid to the hand of her mistress, so our eyes look to the LORD our God, until He is gracious to us."

If we are dependent on God for current mortal life, how much more are we dependent on God for resurrected immortal life. Some may object that dependence on God represents a crutch, a sign of weakness and laziness. While we certainly have important personal responsibilities in life ("working out our salvation with fear and trembling," for example), charges of a crutch mentality fail to recognize just how dependent we are on people outside ourselves. We depend on our mothers to give us birth, our families to name us, our government to build the roads on which we drive and someone (or something) other than ourselves to send sufficient rain and sunlight to sustain the earth and grow the vegetation that feeds us. Are we guilty of a crutch mentality in each of these examples, and many others we could list? No, in each area of dependency we express gratitude and acknowledge our interconnectedness with others. If we have depended on the grace and good will of others for the basic necessity of life, why not embrace dependency on Jesus' death and resurrection as God's means of escalating life into resurrected immortality.

In another example of our dependency on God for life, Bruce Waltke, writing in *An Old Testament Theology*, argues one purpose of the fall narrative in Genesis 3 is to reveal our inability to sustain and understand life apart from God. "If Adam fails in the perfect setting of garden paradise without inherited guilt and a depraved nature, how can stiff-hearted Israel keep the Lord's teaching in Canaan, a land known for its debauchery?"[27] Our only hope is for God to raise the dead, give light to our eyes and create a new heart within us. Yet we often place ultimate confidence for progress and growth in objects other than God. Education, family, government, hard work and healthy habits all shape the world in important ways. None of them can raise the dead to life, reverse decay or perfect the human heart.

Fourth, a bold theology of death and resurrection will cause us to re-evaluate our time, values and resources in light of a resurrection eschatology of what lasts. Eschatology is the study of last things, last days or what will last forever. Speaking in 1 Corinthians 13:8-13, Paul writes:

But if there are gifts of prophecy, they will be done away; if there are tongues, they will cease; if there is knowledge, it

---

[27] Bruce Waltke, *An Old Testament Theology*, 255.

will be done away. [9] For we know in part and we prophesy in part; [10] but when the perfect comes, the partial will be done away. [11] When I was a child, I used to speak like a child, think like a child, reason like a child; when I became a man, I did away with childish things. [12] For now we see in a mirror dimly, but then face to face; now I know in part, but then I will know fully just as I also have been fully known. [13] But now faith, hope, love, abide these three; but the greatest of these is love.

In Paul's eschatology, he differentiates between that which will pass away and that which remains. When we fixate on current realities that will pass away and ignore realities that will remain, we are not living with a resurrection value system. Specifically Paul views God's revelation of "the perfect," seeing God "face to face," "knowing fully," and "love" as examples of what will remain and be common place in the resurrected new heavens and new earth. On the other hand, Paul sees prophecy, tongues, partial knowledge, seeing dimly in a mirror as gifts and good things that will eventually cease. It would be foolish, Paul says to the Corinthians, for you to overvalue your spiritual gifts, which will cease in Christ's perfected reality when he returns, and undervalue love, which will remain and abound in heaven.

Other examples of what will pass away include sin (Romans 6:6), death (1 Corinthians 15:26), the temple (Revelation 21:22), marriage (Matthew 22:30), darkness (Revelation 22:5), war (Psalm 46:9), the sea (Revelation 21:1) and our mortal bodies (1 Corinthians 15:50-53). In several cases such as marriage, the temple, our mortal human body and spiritual gifts, God is doing away with good gifts he has given in order to replace them with even better resurrection gifts and immortal realities. If these good gifts will not remain, we should be careful not to idolize them but rather to re-examine God's current purpose for these gifts, since they will not remain.

Likewise as we look at what remains or is given in the immortal resurrected life Jesus has begun, we find love (1 Corinthians 13:13), new bodies--non-decaying, glorious, powerful Spirit-filled bodies (1 Corinthians 15:42-44), good works (1 Corinthians 3:14, 15:58), face to face communion with God (1 Corinthians 13:12), rulership of the earth with Christ (Revelation 20:6), non-biological family (Matthew 12:47-49) and worship (Revelations 7:9-10). Without abandoning God's current created order, these are things we should emphasize and grow in until the return of Christ.

Fifth, a strong theology of death and resurrection will cause a revolution in cultural, philosophical and political Christian thought. As NT Wright has observed, for much of its history, the doctrine of resurrection was regarded as a dangerous and revolutionary doctrine. The Maccabees used it to fuel their revolution against Rome. The Sadducees, Jerusalem temple power brokers of Jesus' day, denied the doctrine of resurrection, at least partly out of fear for the revolutionary action it might incite.[28] People who aren't afraid of death often do bold things. In Hebrews 11:35, the revolutionary logic of death and resurrection led believers to radical behavior. "Women received back their dead, raised to life again. There were others who were tortured, refusing to be released so that they might gain an even better resurrection."

---

[28] In *The Resurrection of the Son of God*, NT Wright demonstrates that immortal bodily resurrection was universally foreign or even derided in the thought and literature of the Greek and Roman world. Likewise the Saduccean power brokers of Jerusalem, who also disbelieved in the resurrection, feared the effect belief in resurrection might have on young upstart revolutionaries who hoped to be raised from the dead if they died fighting Rome.

Aphorisms such as, "you only live once," "what doesn't kill you makes you stronger," (an implicit admission of death's power) and "only death and taxes are certain" all need to be rethought in the aftermath of Jesus' resurrection. How would we live differently if we lived twice, not once? What if even what kills us could make us stronger through resurrection? What if death, taxes and resurrection are certain? Whether facing persecution, embracing martyrdom, refusing to fear political rulers or devoting ourselves to works that will be rewarded at our resurrection from the dead, the doctrine of resurrection transforms how we view contemporary life.

Sixth, a bold proclamation of Jesus' death and resurrection will intensify our expressions of sorrow and celebration in worship. As we saw in chapter 3, biblical Psalms of lament powerfully embody themes of both Jesus' death and resurrection. Jesus himself prayed a Psalm of lament (Psalm 22) on the cross. Through Jesus' death, he sums up, embraces and invites the fellowship of our own individual deaths with himself. Through Jesus' resurrection he embodies, accomplishes and establishes the rhythm of hope and resurrection for us.

In Psalm 18:4-6, as King Saul pursues David to kill him as a political opponent, David laments the nearness of death:

> The cords of death encompassed me, and the torrents of ungodliness terrified me. The cords of Sheol surrounded me; the snares of death confronted me. In my distress I called upon the LORD, and cried to my God for help; He heard my voice out of His temple, and my cry for help before Him came into His ears.

After he has been delivered, David rejoices in Psalm 18:1-3, "I love You, O LORD, my strength. The LORD is my rock and my fortress and my deliverer, my God, my rock, in whom I take refuge; my shield

90

and the horn of my salvation, my stronghold I call upon the LORD, who is worthy to be praised, and I am saved from my enemies." How much more should we, who now know the true Son of David who has tasted death and established resurrection on our behalf, lament the death that surrounds us and rejoice in Jesus' ultimate victory over that death?

On July 20, 2012 James Holmes opened fire in an Aurora, CO movie theatre killing 12 people. As an example of Christ-centered lament in Christian worship, I wrote the Psalm of lament recorded in Appendix 2 and prayed it during the following Sunday's worship service. Recognizing the horror and pain of death, as well as the victory and final word of resurrection is one way Jesus' death and resurrection enrich our worship and encourage us to engage death and brokenness around us.

Chapter 16: Dying and Rising for Others

Resurrection Truth: Christians are called to participate in the death and resurrection process for the sake of other people.

"So then, death is at work in us, but life is at work in you."
2 Corinthians 4:12

For my twenty-second birthday in March of 2002, my wife gave me one of my favorite birthday presents. She took me to a Steven Curtis Chapman concert in Lakeland, Florida. Midway through the concert, Chapman paused to tell the story of Nate Saint and his four missionary friends from the 1957 book *Through the Gates of Splendor*. Nate was a pilot who, with his fellow missionaries and their wives, made contact with the Huaorani Indians of Ecuador. The Huaorani people were known to be fiercely independent and extremely violent toward outsiders. After an initial positive reception by the Huaorani tribe on January 3, 1956, five days later Nate and four of his missionary friends were speared to death by armed Huaorani warriors. The dead missionary's five wives were evacuated from the area. Nate Saint's son, Steve, was five years old at the time.

With the audience sitting on the edge of their seats in horror, Chapman paused the riveting tale, inviting a special guest to continue the story. Onto the stage walked Steve Saint, Nate's surviving son, who was now 51 years old. Steve picked up where Chapman left off, telling how Rachel Saint (Nate's sister and Steve's aunt) along with Elisabeth Elliot (whose husband was one of the 5 murdered missionaries) returned to the Huaorani people 1.5 years later in the summer of 1958. Rachel and Elisabeth reestablished contact with the Huaorani. Seen as less of a threat than the speared male missionaries, the two women worked to translate the

Huaorani language and tell the story of Jesus' death and resurrection.

In the summer of 1961 at 10 years of age, and only 5 years after his father had been speared to death, Steve Saint began living with his aunt Rachel and the Huaorani tribe during his summers. The Huaorani eventually received the gospel, became "God Followers" (in their own words) and changed their tribal name to Waodani, which means "True People." (The newly named "True People" seem to have a close connection conceptually and experientially to the reality of becoming "new humans" through Jesus' death and resurrection.)

In June 1965, at the age of fourteen, Steve Saint was baptized in the Waodani's Curaray River by Mincaye, a Waodani church elder and one of the converted warriors who had speared Steve's father to death. Shocked by the story of death, suffering and reconciliation, the crowd sat dumfounded again as Steve invited a second guest to join him on stage. Out walked Mincaye, a short, joyful Waodani Indian who had killed Steve's father as a young man and was now approximately sixty-seven years old. With Steve Saint translating, Mincaye told how he and his tribe learned from Steve's family the truth of "God's carvings" (the Bible) and turned from their life of violence and murder to the "good trail" of being God followers. Because Mincaye killed Steve's father Nate, after become a God follower, Mincaye adopted Steve as his tribal son. Steve's children, who also spend time with the Waodani people, call Mincaye "grandfather."

The story of death and resurrection spilling over from Nate Saint and his companions to the Waodani people and then back to Nate Saint's surviving family members is not a one-time isolated experience. Saint's story vividly portrays a deeper universal Christian truth. All Christians are called to participate in the death and resurrection process for the sake of others. Scripture reveals that we die and rise with Jesus for the sake of others in at least three ways.

First, we die and rise with Jesus so others can participate in the Lord's comfort, compassion, affection, salvation and restoration. Like a parent who repeatedly lays down and sacrifices their life so their child can receive life and provision, Jesus does the same for us and invites us to do the same for one another. John 6:51 ("The bread also which I will give for the life of the world is My flesh") and Hebrews 2:9 (Jesus died to "taste death for everyone") confirm Jesus embraced death, so all who embrace him can taste eternal life. More foreign to Christ followers is the notion that they too are called to suffer and die with Jesus, so others can receive the benefits of resurrection.

In 2 Corinthians 1:5-7, Paul sees his sufferings with Christ resulting in comfort for the Corinthians:

> For just as the sufferings of Christ are ours in abundance, so also our comfort is abundant through Christ. But if we are afflicted, it is for your comfort and salvation; or if we are comforted, it is for your comfort, which is effective in the patient enduring of the same sufferings which we also suffer; and our hope for you is firmly grounded, knowing that as you are sharers of our sufferings, so also you are sharers of our comfort.

In addition to suffering for the Corinthians, Paul also finds great hope in the fact that the Corinthians share in Paul's sufferings, as well as Paul's comfort through Christ. Paul is describing a two-way symbiotic relationship within the body of Christ that could not be further from isolated individualism.

In 2 Corinthians 6:3-13, Paul embraces and rehearses a catalogue of his sufferings on behalf of the Corinthians (including:

"dying yet behold, we live") in order to stir up in the Corinthians a reciprocal affectionate love:

> Giving no cause for offense in anything, so that the ministry will not be discredited, but in everything commending ourselves as servants of God, in much endurance, in afflictions, in hardships, in distresses, in beatings, in imprisonments, in tumults, in labors, in sleeplessness, in hunger, in purity, in knowledge, in patience, in kindness, in the Holy Spirit, in genuine love, in the word of truth, in the power of God; by the weapons of righteousness for the right hand and the left, by glory and dishonor, by evil report and good report; regarded as deceivers and yet true; as unknown yet well-known, as dying yet behold, we live; as punished yet not put to death, as sorrowful yet always rejoicing, as poor yet making many rich, as having nothing yet possessing all things. Our mouth has spoken freely to you, O Corinthians, our heart is opened wide. You are not restrained by us, but you are restrained in your own affections. Now in a like exchange—I speak as to children—open wide to us also.

Christ's sufferings and death on our behalf are intended to stir up a response of holy love and affection. Paul saw the same principle at work in his sacrifice and sufferings with Christ for the Corinthians.

Surely the fact that Rachel Saint and Elisabeth Elliot returned to the Waodani tribe after men from that same tribe had speared to death their brother and husband, respectively, increased the Waodani's curiosity, if not their openness and affection. The same dynamic can be seen in churches and ministries where members sacrifice, give and suffer boldly for one another, in contrast to churches and ministries where people selfishly guard their turf or pride, refusing to suffer disadvantage. The first group experiences resurrection hallmarks of joy, fruitfulness and love. The second group remains dead and dry, not realizing the affection and blessing that flows from suffering with Christ for one another.

Perhaps most intriguingly, we have a role to play in each other's restoration through suffering wrong and forgiving one another's sins, just as Christ suffered wrong and forgave our sins on the cross. Jesus starkly proclaims in Matthew 6:15, "If you do not forgive others, then your Father will not forgive your transgressions." Illustrating this truth in longer form, Jesus tells the following parable in Matthew 18:23-35:

> For this reason the kingdom of heaven may be compared to a king who wished to settle accounts with his slaves. When he had begun to settle them, one who owed him ten thousand talents was brought to him. But since he did not have the means to repay, his lord commanded him to be sold, along with his wife and children and all that he had, and repayment to be made. So the slave fell to the ground and prostrated himself before him, saying, 'Have patience with me and I will repay you everything.' And the lord of that slave felt compassion and released him and forgave him the debt. But that slave went out and found one of his fellow slaves who owed him a hundred denarii; and he seized him and began to choke him, saying, 'Pay back what you owe.' So his fellow slave fell to the ground and began to plead with him, saying, 'Have patience with me and I will repay you.' But he was unwilling and went and threw him in prison until he should pay back what was owed. So when his fellow slaves saw what had happened, they were deeply grieved and came and reported to their lord all that had happened. Then summoning him, his lord said to him, 'You

96

wicked slave, I forgave you all that debt because you pleaded with me. Should you not also have had mercy on your fellow slave, in the same way that I had mercy on you?' And his lord, moved with anger, handed him over to the torturers until he should repay all that was owed him. My heavenly Father will also do the same to you, if each of you does not forgive his brother from your heart.

NT Wright has explained that the announcement of forgiveness (especially forgiveness outside the temple sacrificial system) was a highly significant act. To the Jews of Jesus' day, forgiving or being forgiven meant more than not being mean, having nice feelings toward another person or letting go of a grudge. From Daniel's prayer in Daniel 9 and other Old Testament passages such as Isaiah 40, the Jews of the intertestamental period and Jesus' day believed God had sent Israel into exile because of their sin and refusal to heed the words of God's prophets.[29]

In other words, they knew they deserved exile, just as all humans deserve exile from God's presence due to our sin. But they asked God to be merciful because of his promises to their forefathers, not because they deserved mercy. So for John the Baptist and Jesus to announce the forgiveness of sins wasn't just a nice gesture. It was the language of restoration from exile, the return of God's presence to be with his people and the end of Israel's hard labor for sin.

In the parable above Jesus tells a story about a king (God) forgiving his subject (us) an impossibly great debt. The king expects his subject to forgive others their much smaller debts as well. When we connect forgiveness (being released from jail) with restoration (being released from slavery in exile), Jesus is ultimately

---

[29] NT Wright, *Jesus and the Victory of God*, 268-274.

telling a story about God's restoration of all things to himself and his expectation that we participate in the restoration of all things by forgiving one another. To refuse forgiveness is to refuse God's work of restoring all things.

If forgiveness is a form of dying to our desire for punishment and revenge, then restoration to right relationship with God and humanity is a form of resurrection. Certainly this is true of Jesus' death on the cross. God's just punishment of our sin died through his Son's death in our place on the cross, so we could be resurrected to uninhibited life in the presence of God. Just as with the timing of our own death and resurrection cycle, we can't manipulate or predict how or when God will use our suffering and death to bring about comfort, affection, restoration and resurrection life in others. But we do know that resurrection (ours and others) cannot happen without suffering and death. The benefits of carrying Jesus death and life in our body extends beyond our selves to others whom we love, sacrifice for, suffer with and forgive.

Second, we die and rise with Jesus in order to have membership and fellowship in God's faithful people. Consider Jesus' words in Matthew 5:11-12, "Blessed are you when people insult you and persecute you, and falsely say all kinds of evil against you because of Me. Rejoice and be glad, for your reward in heaven is great; for in the same way they persecuted the prophets who were before you." Jesus regards persecution and false accusations against believers as a mark of their membership in the fellowship of God's servants the prophets. Our suffering connects us not only to Jesus, but also to God's faithful people in all times and all places.

Paul also sees suffering and death as a bond that connects the Thessalonian Christians to other churches, to Jesus, the prophets and to Paul's band of missionaries. Paul encourages his church in 1 Thessalonians 2:14-15, "For you, brethren, became imitators of the churches of God in Christ Jesus that are in Judea, for you also endured the same sufferings at the hands of your own countrymen, even as they did from the Jews, who both killed the Lord Jesus and the prophets, and drove us out."

James views suffering, patience and endurance as membership hallmarks in the churches under his care. Consider James 5:9-11:

> Do not complain, brethren, against one another, so that you yourselves may not be judged; behold, the Judge is standing right at the door. As an example, brethren, of suffering and patience, take the prophets who spoke in the name of the Lord. We count those blessed who endured. You have heard of the endurance of Job and have seen the outcome of the Lord's dealings, that the Lord is full of compassion and is merciful.

James views impatience, complaining and a lack of endurance as behaviors that will be punished by the Judge who is standing at the door. Christians who share the fellowship of suffering, patience and endurance with Job and the prophets will receiving blessing, compassion and mercy as "the outcome of the Lord's dealings."

Hallmarks of membership and fellowship in the Christian church are important. Whether it's a prayer of salvation, participation in worship or receiving communion, most churches practice specific rites as signs of membership. Jesus and his apostles taught an additional hallmark of membership in Christ's body that receives infrequent attention today. To belong to Christ's body was to lay down one's life in suffering, patience, persecution and endurance, along with Jesus and the prophets, trusting that God would have compassion, bless and raise us from the dead to great reward.

99

Third, and perhaps most mysteriously, we die and rise with Jesus in order to complete the fullness of Christ's sufferings and usher in his eternal kingdom. Two passages speak to this reality. It is important to recognize that Jesus' work of atonement on the cross is not insufficient or incomplete. But the suffering of God's people is not yet complete, and we will continue carrying Jesus' death and resurrection in our body until God's appointed time. In Revelation 6:9-11, John describes the souls of martyrs who have been killed because of their faithful testimony:

> When the Lamb broke the fifth seal, I saw underneath the altar the souls of those who had been slain because of the word of God, and because of the testimony which they had maintained; and they cried out with a loud voice, saying, "How long, O Lord, holy and true, will You refrain from judging and avenging our blood on those who dwell on the earth?" And there was given to each of them a white robe; and they were told that they should rest for a little while longer, until the number of their fellow servants and their brethren who were to be killed even as they had been, would be completed also.

The suffering and death of Christ's followers, beyond leading to their own resurrection, stirring up affection in other believers or revealing their membership with God's people, is bringing to completion the end of all things and the consummation of Christ's kingdom.

Paul further explains this reality in Colossians 1:24-29:

> Now I rejoice in my sufferings for your sake, and in my flesh I do my share on behalf of His body, which is the church, in filling up what is lacking in Christ's afflictions. Of this church

I was made a minister according to the stewardship from God bestowed on me for your benefit, so that I might fully carry out the preaching of the word of God, that is, the mystery which has been hidden from the past ages and generations, but has now been manifested to His saints, to whom God willed to make known what is the riches of the glory of this mystery among the Gentiles, which is Christ in you, the hope of glory. We proclaim Him, admonishing every man and teaching every man with all wisdom, so that we may present every man complete in Christ. For this purpose also I labor, striving according to His power, which mightily works within me.

Here again we have the theme of "Christ in you," which was so rich in 2 Corinthians 4 with the death and life of Jesus "always" carried in our body. "Christ in you" entails both sufferings and filling up Christ's afflictions. But "Christ in you" also includes "the hope of glory," being made "complete in Christ" and having "His power which mightily works within" us.

We've come full circle. Through repentance and faith all followers of Christ now carry Jesus' death and resurrection life in our bodies. That daily rhythm of death and life is making us a new human, perfecting us, escalating our joy and fruitfulness, giving us comfort and hope, and leading us to ever-deeper fellowship with Father, Son, Holy Spirit and one another. The death and resurrection cycle is scary, counter-intuitive and impossible to embrace apart from the enlivening work of the Holy Spirit. But the daily death and resurrection cycle is God's way forward for us in Christ, and there is no other way. We will either make a life as good as our hands can make it until moth, rust, thieves or time destroy that life, or we will look to God who joyfully raises the dead, both in this life and ultimately in the life to come.

Chapter 17: Throwing the Football

Resurrection Truth: We grow progressively in Jesus' death and resurrection until we die.

"I want to know Christ and the power of his resurrection and the fellowship of sharing in his sufferings, becoming like him in his death, and so, somehow, to attain to the resurrection from the dead." Philippians 3:10-11

What does the future hold? The future holds death and resurrection. As a child I remember listening as adults lamented the hardships of adulthood. "Enjoy your youth," they warned. "Life goes downhill once you become an adult." Adulthood does entail more responsibility and stress. But people who dread adult life miss the power of Jesus' death and resurrection to shape the future. A life remade by death and resurrection holds new mercies, ever-increasing glory and surpassing power.

Death and resurrection with Jesus do not grow old, familiar or boring. To the contrary they grow in depth and value with the passing of time. The Old Testament celebrates, "The steadfast love of the LORD never ceases; his mercies never come to an end; they are new every morning; great is your faithfulness" (Lamentations 3:22-23). If God's mercies, faithfulness and steadfast love were new every morning in the Old Testament, how much more should we expect God's mercy to abound in the New Testament through Jesus' death and resurrection.

In Matthew 11:11 Jesus teaches the greatness of membership in his kingdom. "Truly I say to you, among those born of women there has not arisen anyone greater than John the Baptist! Yet the one who is least in the kingdom of heaven is greater than he." Before his death and resurrection, Jesus claimed to be greater than Jonah, Solomon, the temple, David and the Sabbath (Matthew 12:41-42; Matthew 12:6; Matthew 22:43-45; Matthew 12:8). Jesus' claims of comparative greatness to Old Testament characters and institutions only increase with the power he displayed in death and resurrection. We should therefore expect the mercies of Jesus' death and resurrection in the New Testament age to be new every morning in an even greater way than his mercies in the Old Testament.

Each encounter with death becomes an opportunity for God to raise the dead. Each confrontation with failure becomes an opportunity for God to bring new fruitfulness. Each experience of mourning becomes an opportunity for God to give new comfort. Each trial becomes an opportunity for God to give new victory. Each loss becomes an opportunity to seek the resurrected life of God.

Second, death and resurrection create in us an ever-increasing glory that will never fade. Whereas youth, job security, reputation, financial worth and romantic interests may fade, Jesus' death, resurrection and the life they produce will only increase in glory. 2 Corinthians 3:18 states, "We, who with unveiled faces all reflect the Lord's glory, are being transformed into his likeness with ever-increasing glory, which comes from the Lord, who is the Spirit." According to Paul, the ever-increasing glory of Christ's followers is greater than Moses' glory after seeing God (2 Corinthians 3:7). We possess this greater glory of Christ in the earthen vessel of our body (2 Corinthians 4:7), which is simultaneously wasting away outwardly but being renewed each day inwardly (2 Corinthians 4:16). The cause and source of our ever-increasing glory is Jesus' death and resurrection rhythmically at work in our bodies (2 Corinthians 4:10). Jesus' resurrection at work in us will also cause our earthly, decaying, fading, naked bodies to one day be clothed with an eternal, glorious, powerful, resurrected body, which Jesus already possesses in heavenly glory (2 Corinthians 5:1-5). Everything we place our hope in, outside Jesus' death and resurrection, whether youth, financial security, education, political power or sexual pleasure will fade, decay and disappoint. Jesus' death and resurrection offer the only source of ever-increasing life, joy, glory and love. For Jesus' followers, "what is mortal will be swallowed up by life" (2 Corinthians 5:4), and the swallowing has already begun.

Third, for followers of Christ, death and resurrection offer knowledge and power that surpass any earthly reality we have known. Writing from prison late in his ministry, the Apostle Paul reflects in Philippians 3:10-14:

> [10]I want to know Christ and the power of his resurrection and participation in his sufferings, becoming like him in his death, [11]and so, somehow, attaining to the resurrection from the dead. [12]Not that I have already obtained all this, or have already arrived at my goal, but I press on to take hold of that for which Christ Jesus took hold of me. [13] Brothers and sisters, I do not consider myself yet to have taken hold of it. But one thing I do: Forgetting what is behind and straining toward what is ahead, [14] I press on toward the goal to win the prize for which God has called me heavenward in Christ Jesus.

An apostle of Paul's stature and experience regards himself to still be exploring the power and knowledge of Jesus' death and resurrection.

Clearly the dual realities of dying and rising with Jesus are more than onetime static events for Paul. He again contrasts death and resurrection to placing confidence in the flesh and personal status or accomplishments (Philippians 3:3). Christ is of "surpassing value" to everything else in Paul's life, especially his prior religious accomplishments, which he now regards as rubbish (Philippians 3:8). Resurrection with Jesus also provides the goal, prize and upward call, which frame and motivate Paul's life in the present (Philippians 3:14).

Applying themes from Philippians 3 to contemporary life, followers of Christ should beware of placing confidence in their own flesh, identity or ability apart from God. Fleshly identity and ability pale in comparison to the greatness of Christ at work in us. Recognizing arrogance and despair as two sides of the same coin, believers should also avoid giving up hope when they encounter failure and defeat. The God who raises the dead is greater than our life situations or failures. When our flesh fails, death and resurrection with Jesus abide and continue.

Death and resurrection also mature Jesus' followers over time. Well into his ministry, Paul is still growing as a participant in Jesus' death and resurrection. Believers today can work for the same company, attend the same church, live in the same town for years. But each year they should expect an ever-greater depth, richness and maturity in their life, work and relationships. Last, dying and rising with Jesus provide a goal, prize and destiny worthy of our energy and devotion. In Philippians 3 Paul is straining, pressing on and counting all things lost to attain the heavenly prize of eternal resurrected life in Jesus' presence. Paul does not labor alone, however. He is merely responding to the call and work of Jesus in his life. Philippians 3:13 states, "I press on to take hold of that for which Christ Jesus took hold of me."

Paul's bold words and sacrifice invite us to consider how we are progressively growing in Jesus' death and resurrection. What does the new creation life, the death and resurrection life of Jesus look like in the present? Do we understand the value of this life? Are we willing to take up our cross with Jesus in order to attain to his resurrection from the dead? For all who participate in Jesus' pattern of death and resurrection, Jesus "will transform the body of our humble state into conformity with the body of His glory, by the exertion of the power that He has even to subject all things to Himself" (Philippians 3:21).

Like a spiraling football expertly thrown by an NFL quarterback, the Christian life is taking us somewhere. We progress as followers of Jesus through participation in the reoccurring cycle of death and resurrection and the purposeful spiral toward Jesus' own eternal destiny.   Life in Christ is more than participation in the stationary spin cycle of death and resurrection. Christ's life in us also entails progressive movement toward Jesus' perfected and immortal new humanity in the presence of God the Father.

While all earthly possessions, wealth, youth or health, eventually decay and depreciate over time, only Jesus' death and resurrection in us creates the redemptive spiral of ever-increasing glory, renewed mercies, surpassing power and abundant fruitfulness.   In the words of Jesus, "Do not store up for yourselves treasures on earth, where moth and rust destroy, and where thieves break in and steal. But store up for yourselves treasures in heaven, where neither moth nor rust destroys, and where thieves do not break in or steal" (Matthew 6:19-20). Jesus is our great treasure, possessed in the earthen vessel of our body, uniting us to heaven by his death, resurrection and ascension.

Conclusion

The goal of *Death and Resurrection* has been to advocate a cyclical view of Jesus' death and resurrection for believers and to explore the implications of that view for Jesus' followers and humanity more broadly. This goal may sound unnecessary for a culture saturated with crosses and prominently celebrating Easter as a major holiday. While the symbols of Jesus' death and resurrection remain, their meaning and implications for contemporary life are largely lost and need fresh exploration.

When people hear the truths presented in *Death and Resurrection*, they often ask, "Why haven't I heard this before?" or "Where were these truths when I was experiencing death?" Believer's awareness of these resurrection truths is limited for several reasons. First, as with many teachings of the Old and New Testaments, we can study or discuss them as abstract concepts. The concepts become more relevant after a life situation causes us to wrestle with that teaching at a deeper level. Studying death and resurrection is different than experiencing death and resurrection. Especially in western society, which has driven much of global Christian theological discussion in recent history, we largely hide and downplay death. A society non-conversant about death will have little need or ability to wrestle deeply with the realities of Jesus' death and resurrection in daily life.

Second, Protestants have historically reacted against the "sacrifice of the mass" in Roman Catholic communion theology by emphasizing the one-time nature of Jesus' death and resurrection. While Jesus' death and resurrection are one-time events, our death and resurrection with Jesus are not. Unfortunately, the baby has been thrown out with the bathwater. Protestants have focused so strongly on countering Roman Catholic Eucharistic theology, they've lost sight of dying and rising with Jesus as the central rhythm of the Christian life.

Third, death and resurrection are unsettling and revolutionary doctrines for any culture or society. Sadducees, the Jewish religious and political rulers of Jesus' day, taught against belief in resurrection for a reason. It destabilized their grasp on power.[30] Anyone who has built an institution, family, business or relationship is not eager to see their labor of love die. Dying and rising with Jesus threatens control of what we hold dear. Especially in a society where Christians hold a protective majority or at least a powerful minority politically, socially and culturally, death is undesirable and foreign. We would rather fight to hold or regain our power and prominence than embrace death and look to Jesus for resurrection. Likewise, death and resurrection can't be measured, managed or controlled. They require faith in the love and power of God to raise us from the dead and don't market well in a consumer-based, metrics-driven economy.

Though the truths of Jesus' cyclical death and resurrection at work in believers are often foreign, their rediscovery is essential for Christianity's future life and witness. How will Christians learn to love their neighbor as themselves in a religiously hostile cultural environment apart from daily dying and rising with Jesus? How will Western Christians learn to join their global Eastern and Southern Christian brothers and sisters as martyrs without the death and resurrection of Jesus Christ? How will Christians thrive when their cultural, moral and political influence collapses unless they fully embrace the pattern of death and resurrection? How will individual believers avoid losing their faith from waves of death, loss and failure without Jesus' invigorating death and resurrection at work in our bodies?

---

[30] NT Wright, *The Resurrection of the Son of God*, 131-140.

The centrality of the church's participation in Jesus' death and resurrection, both corporately and individually, is in fresh need of exploration, discussion, experimentation and communal application. When dying and rising with Jesus becomes like inhaling and exhaling air, the church will discover a new way of life that is beautiful, bold, loving, prophetic and redemptive.

Appendix 1: A Childbirth Prayer

Faithful Father of Sarah, Rachel and Hannah. You opened our foremother's wombs to new birth and spoke life to our empty souls. Merciful Son of the Living God, you blessed children who came to you. You brought life to Jairus' daughter and raised from the dead the widow of Nain's son. Blessed Holy Spirit, you caused the virgin Mary to conceive God's Son and gave new birth to a multitude of souls.

We beseech you now Father, Son & Spirit to give the gift of life to your servants (add names of couple here). Just as you blessed Adam and Eve to be fruitful and multiply your image, will you bless (add names here) to be fruitful and multiply the image of Christ in their offspring. We bind (add names here) to Jesus, the author of their salvation. We rebuke any unhealth or hindrance that stands against your creation of life in (add wife's name here) womb. We invite the health and wholeness that flows from your cross Lord Jesus and from life in our Father's presence.

By the death, resurrection and ascension of Jesus Christ we bless you. By the steadfast love of the Father we bless you. By the tender fellowship of the Holy Spirit, we bless you. In the name of the Father, the Son and the Holy Spirit. Amen.

Written by: Rev. Elijah Lovejoy—Church of the Redeemer, Greensboro, NC

Appendix 2: A Modern Psalm of Lament / Appeal for Aurora, CO
(Based on Psalm 59)

Help Lord, wicked men have massacred the innocent.

They plot murder for many days and carry it out in a moment.

We are helpless to stop this wickedness when it happens.

Rise up to deliver the innocent, oh Father of our Lord Jesus Christ.

They wander about killing for pleasure.

They boast of their schemes as they plan mayhem.

They feel no conviction of sin or remorse before you.

But you are not mocked; you say "Vengeance is mine, I will repay."

O Great Shepherd of the sheep, we wait for you to protect us from wolves.

God will bring salvation to his people.

Your servant Paul was a murderer before you converted him and saved your people.

What glory do you receive from a massacre?

Your hand is not weak and your arm is not short.

Overturn the schemes of the devil in our nation.

So people will know the peace of Christ and be fed at your table.

Wash people under the power of Satan in the blood of Jesus instead of the blood of their victims.

O Lord you have broken our chains by the power of Christ.

And the power of Christ will break many more chains.

We will worship you as a holy family and comfort those who grieve.

In you alone is our eternal hope and salvation.

You Jesus are the cornerstone and fortress of our life.

Written by: Rev. Elijah Lovejoy—Church of the Redeemer, Greensboro, NC

Bibliography

Justin Martyr, *First Apology*, Christian Classics Ethereal Library,
    www.ccel.org.

Waltke, Bruce. *An Old Testament Theology: An Exegetical,
    Canonical, and Thematic Approach*. Grand Rapids, MI:
    Zondervan, 2007.

Wright, NT. *Jesus and the Victory of God*. Minneapolis, MN: Fortress
    Press, 1997.

Wright, NT. *Paul and the Faithfulness of God*. Minneapolis, MN:
    Fortress Press, 2013.

Wright, NT. *The Resurrection of the Son of God*. Minneapolis, MN:
    Fortress Press, 2013.

Made in the USA
Columbia, SC
27 May 2021

38589309R00065